MAKING
AUSTR
RIGHT
WHERE TO FROM HERE?

Judith Sloan, Brendan O'Neill, Gary Johns, Jim Molan, Roger Franklin,

Rebecca Weisser, Graeme Haycroft, James Allan, Kerryn Pholi

Jeremy Sammut, Lorraine Finlay, Peter Kurti, Steven Kates, Alan Moran

EDITED JAMES ALLAN

Published in 2016 by Connor Court Publishing Pty Ltd

Connor Court Publishing Pty Ltd
PO Box 7257
Redland Bay QLD 4165
sales@connorcourt.com
www.connorcourt.com
Phone 0497-900-685

Printed in Australia

ISBN: 978-1-925501-35-3

Cover design: Maria Giordano

Front cover cartoon: © Bill Leak, used with permission

Table of Contents

Introduction

This book is the result of a phone call from Anthony Cappello of Connor Court publishing not long after the July 2016 federal election. The Coalition had run what, on any account, was a lacklustre campaign. Mr. Turnbull did not fight them on the unions, or on the boats, or on the need for significant government spending cuts. He certainly didn't don Tony Abbott-like togs and fight them on the beaches. Instead, the Liberal Party made Mr. Turnbull himself the focus of much of the campaign, and mouthed vapid slogans about 'innovation' at pretty near every opportunity. The National Party honourably excepted, that is where the right side of politics chose to fight them in the first post-Tony Abbott coup election. The results were far from pretty. Despite the loss of some million or so former supporters the Coalition did eventually scrape home with a one seat majority in the House, but with even more independents in the Senate. It was far from clear that the supposed or nominal cause for this July 2016 double dissolution election, the Australian Building and Construction Commission ('ABCC') Bill, would end up being passed by the Senate. At the time of writing it is still unclear.

So Anthony picked up the phone and asked me what I thought of the idea of editing a book that would bring together some of this country's leading right-of-centre writers who would then, in the light of the current political state of affairs in Australia, give the reader their takes on the theme – 'Making Australia Right: Where to from

Here?' My job was to find the writers, give them their instructions, and put together the end result. You are holding that end result in your hands.

The first thing was to find the top notch authors. Then I had to agree a general topic with each, be it defence, health, the economy, the media and all the others that make up the themes of the thirteen chapters of this book. After that, and in keeping with the general philosophical approach of many of us on the right, I gave each author a very laissez-faire and minimal set of instructions. Take this assigned chapter topic of yours, together with the book's overall theme of 'Where to from here for the right side of politics', and run with it as you see fit. There was no one-size-fits-all mandated approach, no cut-and-paste imposed uniformity. Some authors ended-up being free-ranging, others more narrowly focused. Some looked at how we got to where we are; others were more concerned with where we need to go; some split the difference. What you will find is a variety of treatments on some of the most important issues facing this country. True, the overall tone is not one of bubbling optimism. How could it be with the current state of the Liberal Party in this country? But it does constitute, with the variety of views and approaches of the authors, a sort of handbook for how the right side of politics might get back on track in this country – at least for those of us who do not think that acting as the pale imitation of Labor is the way to go.

The line-up for this book is as follows. Judith Sloan considers the economy; Brendan O'Neill tackles political correctness; Gary Johns writes on inequality; Jim Molan surveys defence; Roger Franklin goes more big picture and explains the causes for his anger at the Liberal Party; Rebecca Weisser examines the media in this country; Graeme Haycroft does the same with industrial relations; I then look at the state of play in our universities; Kerryn Pholi writes on Aboriginal Australia; Jeremy Sammut discusses health; Lorraine Finlay takes on law-making; Peter Kurti delves into religion and the new sectarianism; Steve Kates scrutinizes interest rate policy; and Alan Moran finishes the collection off by looking at energy policy. So fourteen chapters in all, and each one approached in a different way.

What you have here are top people in their fields giving you something you will not find on the ABC, namely an outlook and an analysis that is something other than the bog-standard left-wing perspective that dominates so much of the airwaves, the newspaper columns, what you find on social media – and these days, alas, even what some Liberal MPs will voice inside the party room.

As an added special treat the great Bill Leak, cartoonist for *The Australian* and someone who knows first-hand the lack of will in the Coalition to stand up for free speech in this country, agreed to do the cover of this book.

Addendum

It is too late to mention Donald Trump's US election triumph anywhere but in this introduction and only briefly. The President-Elect's win came after this book had gone into the production process. Yet it is clear that this Trump win is a game-changer on various fronts. I don't mean by that that Prime Minister Turnbull will have warmer relations with a man who is on his side of the political divide. Anyone who watched Malcolm Turnbull's press conference immediately after it was clear that Trump had won would realise that the result was a shock to Turnbull, and highly unwanted. Given some of the things he and members of his Cabinet had said about candidate Trump it is hardly surprising that our Prime Minister looked highly uncomfortable. And anyway, when I said just above that Trump was on the same side of the political divide as our Mr. Turnbull, that is to give an awful lot of benefits of the doubt to our Prime Minister, who looks to me (as far as his personal beliefs go) to be very much a man of the centre left and to share a lot more in common with Hillary Clinton than with Donald Trump. That said, Mr. Turnbull, Ms. Bishop and the Coalition at least burned fewer bridges with the new American President than did Mr. Shorten.

No, what I meant about the election of Mr. Trump being a game-changer was not that but rather that this will affect a lot of policy calls. The whole renewables/climate change rent-seeking industry will find itself highly vulnerable if Mr. Trump does as he promised and pulls out of the Obama-EU designed Paris climate accord (which was specifically designed NOT to be a treaty because Mr. Obama could not have gotten it through the US Senate). So if Mr. Trump pulls out of that, as well as cancelling the funding of UN climate change programs (another promise made by The Donald), as well as green-lighting more energy exploration on government lands (ditto) and revoking all of Mr. Obama's Environmental Protection Agency Executive Orders (ditto), then it is clear that energy costs in the US will come down noticeably. This will be good for many of the working class who voted for Mr. Trump. However, it will make it very difficult for any Australian government to continue energy policies designed to drive up prices (as well as to allow them to indulge in bumper sticker moralising about saving the planet that never goes on to mention that what we do in Australia has literally zero effect on the planet's future temperatures even if tomorrow in Australia we went back to the Stone Age, which is not far off where the Green Party's policies aim to take us).

The Trump win may also, hopefully, have an effect on reducing political correctness. And were he to manage to have Congress enact the tax cuts he proposed, that too would put pressure on other governments, ours included, to do so too – especially as regards company taxes. The Trump win is likely in my view also further to inflame the anger of many former Liberal voters at the leftward and Labor-lite drift of the party under Mr. Turnbull. As of writing, and despite this country's finest political cartoonist being ensnared in them, the government has refused to move against the s.18C so-called hate speech laws in this country. Mr. Turnbull does though now indicate that it is likely that he and the government will probably, assuming all the stars align, hold an inquiry to look into 18C. Jim Hacker and the *Yes Minister* writers would be proud of this response.

At any rate, we shall see how the election of Donald Trump plays out in this country. Meantime all of the contributors to this fine book hope that you enjoy reading it.

James Allan
November 11th, 2016

The Economy

Judith Sloan

Contributing Economics Editor, *The Australian*

Introduction

When it comes to economic policy, the Liberal Party of Australia is no longer a party of the centre-right. Very few Liberal Party parliamentarians believe in the importance of economic freedom. Rather, most are happier to adopt statist-protectionist stances that involve big government and high taxation.

This lack of philosophical commitment to the principles of classical liberalism was on display after the Coalition was narrowly returned to office in the July 2016 election. Explaining why the government didn't have the time to consider any changes to the contentious section 18C of the Racial Discrimination Act, the Treasurer, Scott Morrison, put it this way: "it doesn't help me reverse the deficit, it doesn't help me repay the debt, it doesn't help me get one more person in a job and it doesn't lead to one extra company investing more in Australia, so you can appreciate that it is not at the top of my list."

This is a telling comment for a number of reasons. First, the Treasurer draws a completely false distinction between the pursuit of liberty and sound economic management. And, secondly, it underscores a completely mistaken belief that the government creates jobs.

If we were to believe Morrison, he is somehow in charge of the economy and his only real impediment is people wishing to pursue, in his opinion, peripheral issues. How wrong he is.

Philosophy

It was not too long ago that the right side of politics in Australia had established a settled position on the economy and economic policy. Interestingly, short-term Liberal Prime Minister, Billy McMahon, was a solid thinker on economic policy and was a committed supporter of free trade. But it wasn't until John Howard became Leader of the Opposition and subsequently Prime Minister that the right side's new way of thinking became apparent.

There was an acceptance that the dollar must be floated, that currency controls needed to be removed, the financial system deregulated, the levels of tariffs and other protective devices needed to be reduced and the system of compulsory arbitration in the labour market modified.

The case for government ownership of airlines, banks, telecommunications and other activities was called into question. And the conservative side of politics either actively supported or implemented the privatization of companies such as Qantas, the Commonwealth Bank, the Commonwealth Serum Laboratories and Telstra.

Having opened up private markets to competition, it soon became apparent that the inefficiencies in the delivery of public infrastructure and services would be a serious impediment to achieving better overall economic performance. The so-called

Hilmer reforms involved imposing competitive pressures on the public sector, including through privatization, the requirement of competitive neutrality and the creation of market-like mechanisms covering a range of public sector activities.

There was broad acceptance that the role of government should be confined to clear areas of need, including defence, border protection and the funding of health, welfare and education, at least for the less well-off. Active demand management via Keynesian-type stimulus would be avoided and taxes should be efficient and as low as possible.

The current approach to economic policy

If we fast forward to 2013, we find that adherence to the philosophical position that had been nurtured and accepted during the 1980s, 1990s and the first half of the 2000s had significantly diminished among members of the right side of politics.

Support for free trade had faltered with the newly elected Coalition government supporting the recently established Anti-Dumping Commission, the role of which is to investigate cases of alleged anti-dumping (imports priced below the cost of production) submitted by aggrieved local producers.

A form of protection akin to tariffs, the Coalition had initially sought to strengthen the anti-dumping laws to provide for a reverse onus of proof. Importers would have been required to prove that the prices of their products were equal to or greater than production costs, with the presumption that they were being dumped. Ultimately, this change did not go through, but it does illustrate the fundamental change in economic thinking of the right side of politics.

Similarly, backing for the free movement of capital that had been a hallmark of the Howard years was crimped by the Abbott government, with a series of restrictions imposed on foreign direct investment. In particular, the size of investment in agriculture requiring vetting by the Foreign Investment Review Board was reduced from around $250 million (close to one billion dollars for US and New Zealand investors) to $15 million.

In addition, a series of new rules were created to restrict foreign investment in real estate by non-residents, with the two most recent treasurers, Joe Hockey and Scott Morrison, gleefully ordering the sale of a number of properties purchased by non-residents.

The federal Coalition government's attitude towards product market deregulation was also tested in 2015 when the Queensland parliament passed the Sugar Industry (Real Choice in Marketing) Amendment act. (The Queensland Labor government had not supported the legislation, but it was passed by the Katter Party parliamentarians and an independent member.) The main thrust of the act is to impose single desk selling through Queensland Sugar Limited and to prevent mill owners marketing processed sugar independently.

It was entirely feasible for the federal government to override this legislation by referring the matter to the National Competition Council. Bear in mind that taxpayers and consumers of sugar had already stumped up over $500 million to compensate sugar growers for the deregulation that took place in the 2000s.

But the Cabinet declined to do so and so the sugar industry in Queensland (the vast majority of all sugar is grown in Queensland) is now being slowly and painfully re-regulated. In the meantime, some of the large foreign mill owners have decided to suspend their investment plans that had run into several hundreds of millions of dollars.

To be sure, during 2014 and 2015, a series of decisions were taken by the federal Coalition government to deny financial assistance to businesses seeking taxpayer handouts – SPC Ardmona and Qantas are the best examples. But this resolve to deny corporate welfare did not withstand the pressure to offer a concessional loan to the ailing steelworks, Arrium Pty Ltd, and to place an order to replace a railway line in South Australia for the express purpose of supporting the company.

The three trade agreements – with Japan, Korea and China – signed by the Coalition government are also counter-examples of backsliding on the commitment to free and open trade. Having said this, these agreements are basically about improving market access in particular sectors rather than representing comprehensive free trade agreements.

The bottom line is that the commitment of the right side of politics to competitive markets, free trade, foreign investment and rejection of industry handouts has been sorely tested since the federal Coalition government won office in 2013. And the overall outcome has been extremely disappointing. Faced with the slightest pressure, the political leaders have generally caved in to rent-seekers rather than stand up for the principles of economic freedom the Liberal Party had fulsomely embraced in the 1990s through to the first half of the 2000s.

Government spending

The right side of politics might be expected to support limiting government spending. When it comes to the federal government, we would be able to assume a Coalition government would be wary about crowding out private sector activity or spending money on inappropriate activities that should be undertaken by state or local governments, the private sector or not at all.

Sadly, the right side of politics now seems to be as committed to high government spending as Labor, although the list of priorities is slightly different between the two sides.

If we consider the figures, federal government spending during the Howard-Costello years averaged 24 per cent of GDP. Since the Coalition came to office in 2013, federal government spending has been close to 26 per cent of GDP.

Consider also the Howard government's last year in office. Federal government spending was $272 billion or 23.1 per cent of GDP. Then look at the financial year 2016-17, three years after the Coalition won office. Federal government spending is budgeted to be $445 billion or 25.8 per cent of GDP.

By 2019-20, federal government spending is expected to be over $500 billion or 25.2 per cent of GDP. Note that this fall in the share of federal government spending as a proportion of GDP is mainly driven by optimistic budget assumptions of (nominal) GDP growth.

The point is that the right side of politics now seems either to favour high government spending or is incapable of reducing spending, certainly in absolute terms. Now it might be said that there are certain impediments to the federal government cutting spending even if this were its inclination.

It is certainly true that the composition of the Senate since 2013 has made it difficult for the government to have its savings measures passed. Moreover, there are spending increases baked into various pieces of legislation of the previous Labor government – think higher education, school funding and the National Disability Insurance Scheme – which can only be unwound through legislative amendment.

That said, the Coalition government has shown a clear tendency to increase government spending in areas such as regional and environmental grants as well as making massive spending commitments to defence projects such as locally constructed submarines and ships ($89 billion in ships and submarines over the twenty years from 2016). It has also promised substantially to increase government spending on childcare fee assistance, although there are plans to reduce outlays on family tax benefits to 'pay' for this commitment.

The conclusion to be drawn is that the right side of politics shows very little commitment to reducing government spending, something it has in common with the Labor side of politics. It is just that its priorities for spending are slightly different from Labor's pet projects.

Taxation

We might also expect the right side of politics to support the case for lower taxation. While it is true that the Coalition government is seeking to reduce the rate of company tax over time (it will create a dog's breakfast in the meantime by selectively reducing company tax rates according to the size of the company), overall general government receipts are expected to increase from 23.9 per cent of GDP in 2016-17 to 25.1 per cent in 2019-20.

A great deal of this higher tax take relates to the inherent bracket creep of unindexed income tax scales. While the government announced in the 2016 Budget that a minor adjustment would be made to the second top income tax scale of 32.5 per cent (to apply from a taxable annual income of $87,000 rather than $80,000), this was offset by an additional superannuation taxation grab amounting to $6 billion over four years.

This is notwithstanding the Treasurer's assurance made in 2015 that "the government has made it crystal clear that we have no interest in increasing taxes on superannuation either now or in the future." (Evidently keeping promises is no longer part of the behavioural norms of the right side of politics either.)

The Coalition government also had no hesitation in matching Labor's commitment to increase the rate of excise tax on tobacco products and extending the period of annual hikes in the rate. Between 2017 and 2020, the tobacco excise rate will be increased by 12.5 per cent each year, with the total additional revenue amounting to $4.7 billion.

Any notion that the federal Coalition government is committed to reducing the tax take or, for that matter, reforming the tax system to reduce the distorting impacts on work effort and investment is now completely fanciful. The right side of politics is as committed as Labor to imposing higher taxation overall, although the preferred taxation measures will differ slightly between the two sides of politics.

Structural reforms

Sensing that the Coalition government lacked a coherent strategy in relation to economic management after its narrow re-election in July 2016, the Treasurer Scott Morrison quickly delivered a series of so-called headland speeches.

The second speech was entitled: *Staying the course of economic reform – increasing what we earn.* In a very confused presentation, Morrison argued that Australia's main challenge is somehow to lift "what we earn" by which he means raising the rate of growth of nominal GDP. Nominal GDP is the main driver of taxation revenue.

What he failed to acknowledge is that as a price-taker, Australia has no real scope to alter the terms of trade (the ratio of export to import prices). The only way to lift the rate of growth of nominal GDP is through productivity improvements and higher labour force participation.

It is hard to understand why the Treasurer would not describe the economic policy strategy as one focusing on raising productivity and increasing the rate of workforce participation. Note however that achieving the latter is difficult in the context of locked-in demographic shifts.

The problem with talking about increasing what we earn is that many commentators (and members of the public) would take this to connote efforts by the government to raise more taxation and other revenue.

Notwithstanding this qualification, Morrison made the following sound point: "within this country under the previous Labor government, the prescription being followed in the past GFC world has been to put government at the centre. The focus has been on both monetary and fiscal policy stimulus that at best can only ever bring forward investment rather than create it, as it eventually has to be paid for. This is not a sustainable solution."

He went on to say that: "with monetary policy having exhausted itself and expansionary fiscal policies leaving us with higher taxes and bigger debts, we believe economic policy must take a different path by particularly focusing on lifting the level of private investment in the economy. I have been consistently advocating the need for structural reforms to take priority over the focus on monetary and fiscal stimulus."

Now this is solid analysis. The problem arises from the government's belief that it is practising what is being preached by implementing the so-called 'national plan for jobs and growth'.

The very notion that a government would have a plan underscores the point that it does not have a coherent approach to economic management based on limited government and the principles of economic freedom.

Consider also the elements of the plan – constructing a gas market when the current distortions are the result of government decisions and regulations; the enterprise tax plan (mentioned above) the aim of which is to lower the rate of company taxation over a decade; the massively expensive and delayed National Broadband Network and other infrastructure spending; the re-instatement of the Australian Building and Construction Commission; the ill-considered National Innovation and Science Agenda; the defence industry spending; the responses to the Murray report on the financial sector and the Harper report on competition policy and law; yet another jobs program directed at long-term unemployed young people (the PaTH project); and even higher government spending on childcare.

It would be a brave economist to aggregate these measures, many of which are expensive and likely to fail cost-benefit analyses, and claim that they amount to a structural reform package that is likely to budge the rate of growth of productivity.

Indeed, some of them may well detract from this objective – the commitment by the government to alter the misuse of market power test in the Competition and Consumer Act to an effects test is both controversial and could more easily kill off innovation rather than promote it. (After all, this section is being altered to appease the National Party on the basis that farmers need to be protected from the market power of the supermarket chains.)

Conclusion

In theory, we might expect the right side of politics to approach economic policy using the principles of economic freedom as the guiding framework. Government spending restricted to a small range of functions; attempts to reduce government outlays; lower taxation based on a package of measures with the least distorting impact; and minimising the impact of government regulation on businesses and citizens.

Sadly, this is not how the federal Coalition government, first elected in 2013, approaches the tasks at hand even if there are occasional hints of sound policy thinking. The very idea of having a 'national plan for jobs and growth' does indicate that politicians from the right side of politics have fallen into the trap of thinking that (a) a government should have a plan and (b) it is capable of imposing its will on the economy. In reality, economic outcomes are the result of the atomistic behaviour of millions of consumers and producers and all governments need to acknowledge this.

If this were not tragic enough, the right side of politics now seems to have turned its back on free trade and unrestricted foreign investment. Clear protectionist tendencies have come to the fore and are being reflected in various policy initiatives such as restrictions on foreign investment in agriculture and support for the re-regulation of the sugar industry. And the decision to fund the construction of over-priced and possibly defective submarines and ships locally is further indication of an inward looking approach to economic policy.

The end result of this reversion to poor economic policy – the right side of politics had very poor credentials on this front prior to the mid-1980s – will be continued sluggish growth in productivity, underemployment in the labour market and budget repair that is very difficult to achieve.

In all likelihood, some sort of crisis – another global financial crisis, Australia's loss of its AAA credit rating – will be needed before some sort of sense prevails in relation to economic policy. It will also require a visionary leader who can explain what is required and that there will likely be short-run costs. But the alternative is for the country to muddle on, while slowly losing international competitiveness with relative living standards slipping. This is surely not a very palatable option.

Political Correctness

Brendan O'Neill

Editor of *Spiked Online* and a columnist for *The Australian*

"Political correctness" is a quaint phrase to describe a sinister system of censorship. Indeed, this phrase, especially its eye-roll-inducing acronym "PC", which is only ever used as a term of abuse against those who are myopically obsessed with policing people's use of language, is not up to the task of capturing the seriousness of the situation we find ourselves in today. Instances of "PC" usually induce laughter, mockery, as we collectively shake our heads over "loopy lefties" who want to rewrite nursery rhymes or scrub the word "blackboard" from the historic record lest its utterance ever offend someone who happens to have black skin. But there is little amusing in what the rise of PC fundamentally represents, which is the intensification of the moral policing of thought, ideology, everyday conversation and interpersonal relations. It is time to understand that PC is more than the humorously excessive behaviour of fun-lite feminists and academics, and rather represents perhaps the most thorough system of speech control of modern times.

Of course PC deserves the mirth-filled ridicule it receives. When the BBC airs an updated version of A Midsummer Night's Dream that excises the "sexist" line spoken by Helena to Demetrius – "treat me as your spaniel" – that requires mockery. That sort of speech might have been "standard in the 1590s", said the writer of the Beeb's bastardised version of A Midsummer Night's Dream, "[but] it is not the standard now". We indeed have a duty to laugh at the arrogance of BBC suits who imagine 400-year-old classics should be rewritten to suit their 21st-century sensibilities. When PC publishers bring out books of children's songs with all mentions of booze and mayhem removed, as the British publishing charity Bookstart did in 2009, again mockery is a must. Bookstart took the PC scissors to such ditties as "What Shall We Do With the Drunken Sailor?", in which it replaced "drunken sailor" with "grumpy pirate" (to discourage interest in alcohol) and "Stick him in a bag and beat him senseless" with "Tickle him till he starts to giggle" (to discourage acts of violence). That is the work of a creepily Orwellian mindset – stick bad nursery rhymes down the "memory hole" – and it deserves the tag of "political correctness gone mad".

Likewise, campus crusaders' insistence on policing everything from old works of literature (some of which now come with trigger warnings if they contain references to sexual assault) to everyday conversation between people of different races (which is apparently a minefield of unwitting "racial microaggressions") deserves to be "called out", to use one of the PC lobby's own favourite phrases. It is right to mock LaTrobe University in Australia for introducing trigger warnings on discussions of everything from mental health to "body image, eye contact, food, and insects". Reading Kafka's The Metamorphosis in class? Then you'd better issue a trigger warning about monstrous insects so that insect-sensitive students can flee the room. This is indeed mad, and an invitation to intellectual paralysis, since surely every book ever written could cause offence to someone. When publishers bring out a new edition of Mark Twain's Adventures of Tom Sawyer and Huckleberry Finn with its 219 uses of the word "nigger" taken out, as happened in 2011, that warrants ridicule, too. And when the London Museum airbrushes the cigar from Winston Churchill's mouth in a massive picture celebrating Churchill's life – as it did in 2010 – that must also be laughed at. How ironic, and, yes, amusing, that the British political leader who had so many tussles with Stalin should fall victim to Stalin-style airbrushing in his very own country. Where Stalin had former comrades erased from old photos, 21st-century, PC Britain erases cigars from Churchill's gob in old photos, lest anyone foolishly think: "Churchill smoked, so maybe smoking ain't so bad." Censorship for the people's good: the hallmark of PC.

And yet as we laugh at "PC gone mad", we must also appreciate the depth of what is occurring here, and the unprecedented nature of the scope of censorship in the PC era. There is a danger that mockery of PC, though essential, is distracting from an analysis of how we got to a situation where books are casually rewritten, photos are doctored, offensive language and ideas are expunged from the academy, and even nursery rhymes – nursery rhymes! – are reworked in the name of controlling what people hear and see and in the process taming their worst instincts. That is, how we got to a situation where the sort of insatiable, society-wide censorship that shocked us when it was being done in the Soviet bloc in the mid-20th century has now become commonplace in the post-Berlin Wall West. The focus on the most ludicrous manifestations of PC risks overlooks PC's thorough colonisation of almost every aspect of intellectual, political and social life in the West. It's time to ensure that the mockery of PC is accompanied by a deeper analysis and more profound challenge to the moral pretensions of the PC lobby, and their presumption of the Stasi-like right to govern and correct our every utterance, conviction and interpersonal engagement.

Policing Behaviour

One of the most difficult things about developing a thoroughgoing critique of PC is working out what PC is. Many people deny it even exists. Others say it is merely "institutionalised politeness", a shift from an era in which sexist speech and the use of phrases like "coloured people" was seen as acceptable to one in which it is not – and who could be opposed to that? As the author Barbara Gallagher claims, "the original intent of political correctness" was "good" – "to encourage tact and sensitivity to others' feelings around issues of gender, race, religion, sexual orientation, physical disabilities, and such". Others say the tag of "PC" is a right-wing caricature of leftists who are merely earnest, and even good-natured, not wicked or censorious. Tackling PC is difficult when its very existence is doubted by many, or when it is treated as evidence of social progress for women and minority groups.

To my mind, a pretty good approach to PC, or at least a starting point for understanding both its origins and its now terrifying scope in public and private life, is to see it as perhaps the clearest expression of the shift of politics in recent decades away from addressing public and economic concerns towards correcting the thought and behaviour of individual citizens. Aidan Rankin, in his interesting book *The Politics of the Forked Tongue*, described PC as a development that springs from the political turn from the "macro" to the "micro". There has been a palpable move from "broader concerns with the economy and society towards far more trivial issues involving the way people lead their lives", says Rankin. Indeed, the story of Western politics over the past few decades has been the throwing open of more and more areas of private life to the diktats and policing of officialdom and various other "expert" groups. This can be glimpsed in everything from the rise of the nanny state, to the growth of nudge policies (designed to "nudge" people towards eco-cleaner, healthier behaviour), to the spread of hate-speech legislation designed to control what we say. PC should be seen in this vein. In this sense, the "political" part in the phrase "political correctness" can be misleading: yes, PC governs aspects of political speech, but more fundamentally it speaks to, and comes from, and energises, the shrinking of politics, and the turn of politics from governing infrastructure to governing minds and bodies.

What Rankin refers to as the turn from the "macro" to the "micro" ultimately represents a usurping of one of the central ideals of the Enlightenment: namely that officialdom should concern itself with the "outward" rather than "inward" areas of life. In his 1689 'Letter Concerning Toleration', one of the most important documents of the Enlightenment, John Locke sought to "settle the bounds" between what our rulers should and should not do. Officialdom should concern itself only with "civil interests", he argued, not with an individual's "inward" existence: his soul, mind, religion. "The business of laws is not to provide for the truth of opinions", argued Locke, "but for the safety and security of the commonwealth and of every particular man's goods and person". If Locke, as many thinkers insist, is the modern founder of liberalism, then the turn in recent decades from a politics concerned with the "commonwealth" to one that legislates for "the truth of opinions" — through new forms of legal censorship, incessant public-health interference, lifestyle policing, and so on — surely captures the crisis of liberalism. Ours is an era that muddies "the bounds" set by Locke and opens up our inward lives to external intervention. PC is not a creed apart, a strange and amusing blot on contemporary society; rather, it is the very essence of this broader creeping colonisation of inward life.

This is why PC can seem so widespread and influential, correcting speech and ideas everywhere from universities to publishing houses to the interaction between citizens who are increasingly uncertain about what can and cannot be said: not because it is a strong, well-founded ideology, but because it is the beneficiary of an already existing erasure of the bounds between government business and the inward life of citizens. In his 2006 book *The Retreat of Reason*, Anthony Browne noted the striking march of PC "through every nook and cranny of national life, leaving nothing untouched"; he says this was "helped by the fact there is little competing ideology". Yes, it is the decline of politics as we knew it, and its replacement by what the British Labour Party calls "the politics of behaviour" – a post-ideological "new politics [that] is about moderating behaviour and re-establishing the social virtues of self-discipline" – that has nurtured PC. This new politics explicitly calls into question both the capacity and the right of individuals to self-governance, to shape their behaviour and their beliefs as they see fit, free from the interference of others. That is, it weakens, or rather is built upon the weakness of, the ideals of liberalism. PC is the corollary of the West's new governance of inward life, seeking to colonise the realms of thought and speech in a similar way to how the public-health lobby has assumed authority over the realms of health, parenting, environmental behaviour, and so on.

The New Thought Control

And the consequence is that barely any area of thought and speech is free from either legal censorship or social, elite pressure to eschew eccentricity of thought and conform to what is considered the "politically correct" view. Some historians of PC note the origins of the phrase in radical left-wing circles. In Paul Berman's 1992 book, *Debating PC: The Debate over Political Correctness on College Campuses*, it is pointed out that "politically correct" was "originally a phrase on the Leninist left to denote someone who steadfastly toed the party line". In January 2016, an essay in the Washington Post said the term "politically correct" "began to circulate in American Communist circles in the 1930s and 40s", and was used to mean "the proper language to use, or the proper position for a member of the US Communist Party to take". However, this reflection on the Communist origins of the term PC can be misleading, since it presents PC as a strictly ideological form of censorship hanging over from the 20th century, when in truth it is something possibly worse: a new censorship we might call "therapeutic censorship", unanchored by ideology and therefore more unwieldy and insatiable than any censorships that existed in the last century.

The most striking thing about PC is the breadth of its speech control – its spread into all "nooks and crannies", as Browne puts it. The British comedian Stewart Lee calls PC "institutionalised politeness", merely a creed for encouraging nicer ways of speaking among different groups in society. In truth, PC corrects speech of almost every variety. It has nothing to do with niceness, and rather creates the space for ideological censorship, political censorship, religious censorship, artistic censorship, literary censorship, and even conversational censorship. Censorships of old may have been more violent and unforgiving than PC – mercifully, no one is burnt at the stake for singing "What Shall We Do With the Drunken Sailor?" – but they were not as all-encompassing as PC is.

Far from merely correcting racial or social impoliteness, PC explicitly punishes political opinion. The PC elite's ever-broadening definition of "hate speech" has led to certain moral and religious views being collapsed together with prejudice and suffering censure as a consequence. The punishment of Andrew Bolt under Section 18C of the Racial Discrimination Act was a clear case of the use of PC strictures ostensibly against offensive and anti-social speech to discipline those who merely hold unpopular political views, in this case that it is wrong to have an ever-widening definition of Aboriginal heritage. Likewise with the Queensland of University Technology students being threatened under Section 18C merely for expressing a political view on the segregation of classrooms by race. The investigation of *The Australian's* cartoonist Bill Leak over his image of an Aboriginal father who doesn't know the name of his troubled son is the latest clear example of the race law being used to clamp down on political statement and intellectual critique.

Across Europe, too, laws that are justified as a means of "institutionalising politeness" – to use Stewart Lee's celebration of the intent of PC – have been deployed in service of political and moral censorship. The Swedish pastor given a one-month suspended prison sentence for describing homosexuality as a "tumour" on society, and thus breaking the PC code against criticism of gays; the former French actress, Brigitte Bardot, fined 30,000 Euros for ridiculing the "barbaric" way in which Muslims kill animals for meat; the French novelist Michel Houellebecq taken to court for describing Islam as "the most stupid religion"; the Scottish football fan given a four-month prison sentence for singing an anti-Catholic song on his way to a football game, and therefore breaking the law of Scotland's Offensive Behaviour at Football Act; the hard-right bloggers Pam Geller and Robert Spencer being banned from entering Britain on the basis that their criticisms of Islamism are not "conducive to the public good"… in each of these cases, and many others besides, laws or codes against offensive or discriminatory speech – that is, against non-PC speech – have limited the expression of what are in fact strongly held political and moral views.

PC's enforcement of "politeness" nurtures artistic and literary censorship, too. Art or artists judged offensive suffer under PC. In 2014, the Barbican in London closed down an art exhibition that featured black actors in cages after certain black-community groups described it as "offensive" and "humiliating". Also in 2014, the

Swedish artist Dan Parks was jailed for six months for producing artworks that included racist caricatures of black and Roma people. His artworks were later pulped by the state. In the Middle Ages, European officials burnt heretical books; now they destroy un-PC art. The hounding out of Australia of the Georgian opera singer Tamar Iveri, after it was discovered she had posted a homophobic comment on her Facebook page, confirmed PC's rehabilitation of the Soviet-era conviction that only artists with the right views may perform in public. PC's insistence on sensitivity to Muslims in particular has led to a huge amount of artistic self-censorship. The northern English Hull Truck Theatre Company rewrote a play following the Danish-cartoons controversy in the mid-2000s, changing a Muslim character to a Rastafarian; the Barbican excised sections from its production of Tamburaline the Great for fear of offending Muslims; and London's Royal Court Theatre cancelled a reading of an adaptation of Aristophanes' Lysistrata because it was set in a Muslim heaven. These cases speak to one of the most insidious impacts of the growth of PC and its demonisation of certain views: the chilling of artistic freedom and experimentation, which acts as a permanent invitation to self-censorship in the name of avoiding the giving of offence.

In the literary world, PC concerns have led to Islam-critical books being delayed or simply not published. Twain has been tampered with, Shakespeare rewritten, and the works of Enid Blyton have been subjected to what are ominously referred to as "sensitivity revisions". So "housemistress" is changed to "teacher"; "dirty tinker" has become "traveller"; and the naughty boy is not given a "good spanking" but a "good talking-to". This is literary censorship, of the Orwellian variety, where inconvenient ideas or words from the past are plunged down the memory hole – not in the name of The Party but in the service of the PC goal of eradicating offensive language and protecting individual sensibilities. Trigger warnings on books in many universities – such as *The Great Gatsby* (TW: mentions sexual assault) and Ovid's *Metamorphoses* ("TW: contains offensive material that marginalises student identities", says Columbia University) - are not literary censorship as such, but they do stigmatise literature through depicting its potential offensiveness as a threat to the mental health and self-esteem of readers.

Such instances of political, moral, artistic and literary censorship and self-censorship give the lie to the notion that PC merely encourages good manners. In truth it has nurtured a vast new system of interference in the written and spoken word. Worse, it is spreading into interpersonal speech, too, and even into thought itself. The rise of the idea of "microaggressions" on American campuses, now spreading to other academies in the Western world, shows how far the PC lobby wishes to interfere into intimate, daily chatter. A microaggression is defined as an unwittingly racist or hurtful comment, such as asking a person of colour "where are you from?" At UCLA, even the phrase "America is a land of opportunity" has been redefined as a microaggression on the basis that it implies "race or gender does not a play a role in life successes". The spread of speech codes governing how we address one another cuts to the heart of the warped PC mission, or at least its logical conclusion: that even private conversation must be policed, and all of us must adhere to a new etiquette when we speak to other human beings. The end result can only be social paralysis, a crippling uncertainty in relation to the very basics of human engagement, especially between people of different races – so much for PC's claim to be making society more racially tolerant.

Can PC go even further than policing conversation? Yes. And it is. It is moving into the mind itself. The sacking of Sydney University's Barry Spurr for "offensive" things he said in utterly private emails suggests that even the most intimate parts of our thoughts and expression now fall under the remit of PC. In response to a similar controversy over private conversations in the US, a *Washington Post* writer captured the tyrannical endpoint of PC when she said: "If you don't want your words broadcast in the public square, don't say them... Such potential exposure forces us to more carefully select our words and edit our thoughts." In short, the PC culture of humiliation is a good thing because it puts immense pressure on people not to utter what is in their minds, and fundamentally to alter what is in their minds – to "edit their thoughts". This policing and punishment even of private thoughts and speech also runs directly counter to Enlightenment ideals. Following the calamity of The Inquisition, the great 17th-century English jurist Edward Coke pointed the way to a new, more liberal era when he said: "No man, ecclesiastical or temporal, shall be examined upon the secret thoughts of his heart, or of his secret opinion." Today, however, men, and women, are examined upon their secret thoughts and private and public opinions - not by the Spanish Inquisition but by a new tyrannical system deceptively referred to as "institutionalised politeness".

Towards a New Enlightenment

PC is a counter-Enlightenment. Both its muddying of the bounds between the business of government and the citizen's inward life and its harassment and disciplining of those who hold certain views powerfully undermine the liberal, humanist outlook that emerged from the ashes of Inquisitorial intolerance. Its relentless spread is not down to the hard work of its enforcers or the "march of pinkos" through the institutions, as too many on the right would have us believe, but rather to the general weakness of liberal, enlightened values across the modern West. Anthony Browne is right when he says PC's occupation of society's "nooks and crannies" speaks to the glaring absence of a "counter-PC movement". Where has been the defence of freedom of thought and speech and of the capacity of all autonomous adults to negotiate public and private life without needing official assistance? Such a defence has been meek at best. For this reason, many of the right-wing critics of PC would do well to look in the mirror occasionally, for it has been their failure to defend liberal or traditional values from the 1960s onwards that has fuelled the opportunistic spread of a new and unforgiving moral etiquette. PC is ultimately parasitical on the corrosion of the West's sense of itself and its crisis of enlightened, democratic thought.

The key justification for PC censorship is not the need to protect a party, ideology or godhead from ridicule, but rather to protect the individual from offence. This therapeutic censorship takes as its starting point the idea of the fragile individual, lacking the moral independence and intellectual resolve required for public life and thus needing the scaffolding of therapy to help him through the worlds of speech, ideas and interpersonal relations. The Enlightenment view of the individual was a free-willed, reasoned creature, deserving of and capable of freedom, as captured in Locke's advice that men should live by "the light of their own reason" rather than "blindly resign themselves up to the will of their governors". PC does the precise opposite of this, inviting us to surrender to the better wisdom of our rulers and the political set, and to resist the darkness of our own warped, probably racist reason. That's because its starting point, as with this era's politics of behaviour more broadly, is a vision of the diminished individual, unreasoned, vulnerable, requiring guidance through every stage of life.

In this sense, it benefits no one to turn the discussion of PC into a right/left issue, with the right consistently describing PC as "cultural Marxism" or "militant leftism". A more intelligent right would surely recognise that PC represents, not the ascendancy of the left politics of class and conflict, but its demise and its replacement by a new cloying and censorious politics of identity that emphasises people's incapacity over their capacity, and their biological differences over their shared material interests. PC is pushed mostly by ostensible leftists, yes, but that only confirms the historic crisis of the left's old aim of reimagining and remaking society, and its adoption of the new, infinitely narrower goal of fixing ordinary people and their bad morals and ill health. In essence, PC represents a challenge to the old moral foundation of both left-wing and right-wing politics in their earliest incarnations: that is, the idea of reasoned individuals who have the necessary moral and mental equipment to engage in politics and society and think for themselves. This idea is what must be restored if we are truly to tackle PC and its stranglehold over politics, education and, increasingly, our minds and souls.

Inequality as the Means of Progress

Gary Johns

Columnist for *The Australian* newspaper and a Director of The Australian Institute for Progress

A march back through the institutions

The Right believes in less taxation and less government interference in people's lives: in short, liberty. But in a world where more Australians vote for their money than work for it, and the constituency beholden to government for benefits and jobs is expanding, the constituency for winning votes with tax cuts and deregulation is diminishing. Selling stringency and insecurity is not going to win elections. Rather, the Right have to advance a cultural debate in conjunction with the economic debate. The Right have to promote a discussion that has, at worst, no cost to the budget, and builds a constituency. It is not a case of 'bread and circuses', of creating diversions, but of the necessity to build a constituency that trusts government to be less intrusive. It is a necessity to overcome the shameless bribery that all politicians indulge in, but especially from the Left. There is never enough of someone else's money to provide equality for all.

Getting government off voter's backs is not very appealing to a very large number of voters. Achieving greater liberty is going to take a reinvigoration of ideas. A political program to inspire and to change the political culture in Australia to one more amenable to liberty will require both economic and cultural conversations. Taking a leaf from the Left handbook, I would suggest a march back through the institutions. The long march through the institutions, a slogan coined by 1960s German student activist Rudi Dutschke, possibly inspired by Antonio Gramsci, described his strategy for establishing the conditions for a socialist economy and a social revolution. The social revolution contained elements that are liberal and benign, equality for women for example. Unfortunately, such reasonable aspects have become burdensome when encrusted with welfare provisions. The Right need a similar strategy for a liberal economy and the social revolution, without the bill.

The economic side of the bargain, less tax, and less regulation, is familiar. The social side less so. The Right support self-reliance. In Australia, and elsewhere, self-reliance has been undercut in two ways: the burgeoning welfare state and, more recently, the restriction of free speech to protect those with certain 'attributes' such as race, religion, gender, sexual orientation and so on. The greatest example of this is the overweening and illiberal tendency of so-called progressives to conflate their demands for identity rights with liberty. Responding to these dual threats may not, however, mean fewer regulations. Libertarians make this mistake. In some instances, where access to welfare is concerned, more regulations, or more accurately, more obligations, may be necessary.

Debunk inclusive prosperity

The long march must commence by demolishing the Left's (current) big lie. Labor's recent variation on an old theme – equality – is 'inclusive prosperity'.[1] Derived from analyses such as those of the French Marxist Thomas Piketty, it is the belief that inequality stunts growth.[2] The Left now argue that not only is inequality unfair but that it is uneconomic. How creative is that? The recipe ensures that not only should government interfere in people's lives, but also that those dependent on government should receive its largesse without question because it is good for the economy. The recipe is patently wrong, and readers should study Angus Deaton, the 2015 Nobel Prize winner in economics, for the many reasons why. Deaton's recent book on the subject of inequality is the story of progress, cast as "the endless dance between progress and inequality, about how progress creates inequality, and how inequality can sometimes be helpful – showing others the way, or providing incentives for catching up – and sometimes unhelpful – when those who have escaped protect their positions by destroying escape routes behind them".[3] Only in the latter sense can inequality be said to be harmful.

The powerful and wealthy in Australia have rarely set out to destroy escape routes by, for example, destroying public schools and public hospitals. The entire public school system and the generous public support for private schools, along with public hospitals, Medicare and the Pharmaceutical Benefits Scheme, and more recently the National Disability Insurance Scheme, are the testament. It appears, however, if one listens to the Left, that these are insufficient to achieve inclusive prosperity. It appears, alas, the goal can only be reached by having the 'caring professions' labour with taxpayer's money to the point where every person has the opportunity for similar outcomes to all others. The fact that inequality endures for perfectly good reasons, such as

---

[1] Michael Cooney, 2016. "Inequality: The facts and the future." *Chifley Research Centre Inclusive Prosperity Commission*.
[2] Thomas Piketty, 2014. *Capital in the Twenty-First Century*. Mass: Cambridge University Press.
[3] Angus Deaton, 2013. *The Great Escape: Health, Wealth, and the Origins of Inequality*. Princeton University Press, xiii.

the unequal distribution of brains or brawn, and motivation, is of no account.

The never-ending struggle for equality, in combination with democracy's vulnerability to running large public sector deficits, ensures that Piketty's 'destructive program' eats away at the heart of many western democracies.[4] Left politicians use it to provide cover for their constituents' needs and desires. Right politicians use it to compete with the Left by buying votes among their preferred constituents. For Labor politicians buying votes by recirculating taxation dollars in benefits and programs comes easy. They are, after all, pursuing their goal of inclusive prosperity. For the Right, the goal is more difficult because they appear to be against inclusive prosperity. The Right must learn to embrace inequality as the means of progress. They must argue the case that equality means taking the earnings of good people. They must argue the case that equality rewards rent seekers. They must argue the case that equality provides cover for those who do not share liberal values. Here are openings for the Right to develop a political strategy.

A long road back

Australia may not be in the parlous position of European welfare states, but it is headed in the wrong direction. As Tony Makin and Julian Pearce argue, "there has been a major deterioration in the [Australian] federal government's net worth position since the fiscal stimulus response to the GFC." Also, an enduring cause of public debt is that Australian general government real per capita payments and receipts (in 2011-12 dollars) have risen from $6,000 in 1972

---

[4] George Reisman, 2014. *Piketty's Capital: Wrong Theory, Destructive Program.* TJS Books California.

to $16,000 projected in 2020.[5] Weaning Australians from welfare is going to take strong medicine. The medicine would consist of strong social and cultural messages to reclaim important institutions. But, there is no single response, in each case a different formula is applied.

The Right need to work many responses to the Left's hegemony in many key institutions, but here are three examples: free speech must be tied to national security as part of the immigration debate: strong obligations should be imposed on social security recipients in a bid to break intergenerational dependence: and, parent purchasing power must be used in school selection to break the Left's monopoly on the curriculum. The general approach could be summed up as 'strong choices, strong obligations'. At present Australian public policy seems to be characterised by 'few choices, weak obligations'.

Free speech tied to security and immigration

Tony Abbott, now on the backbench, has admitted that he was wrong not to proceed with his promised amendments to section 18 C of the Racial Discrimination Act when he was Prime Minister. Apparently, he failed to proceed because of lobbying by a number of Liberals who held seats in the western suburbs of Sydney and were fearful of the Muslim vote. The outrageous case of the Queensland University of Technology students who were excluded from an 'indigenous space' and then sued because they were indignant, should strengthen the pressure to amend the RDA. The Right has to join those Senators who wish to revisit section 18 C to remove the words 'offend' and 'insult'. The Right could, of course, go the whole way and also remove the words 'humiliate' or 'intimidate', but it might be best to take the easier path.

---

[5] Tony Makin and Julian Pearce, 2016. 'Fiscal Consolidation and Australia's Optimal Public Debt.' Unpublished Griffith Business School Griffith University.

More than this, however, the free speech debate must be explicitly linked to immigration and secure borders. Free speech has to be part of a bigger agenda. It must move from a debate for academics to a debate for the public. John Howard won the 2001 election assisted by the sentiment, "we will decide who comes to this country and the circumstances in which they come". Tony Abbott won the 2013 election by promising, among other things, to "stop the boats". Both were strong on border protection. In each case, there was a strong constituency for security.

Part of secure borders is an immigration policy that explicitly assesses the risk associated with the religious and political views of any potential immigrant. The Right should also insist on an explicit policy of integration to replace multiculturalism, which has become a political front for ethnic and religious groups to organise around group demands. This debate must be tied to security. There is a constituency for security against terrorism and terrorism in Australia has one source: Islam. The source of the threat to Australians may be political, an anti-western mindset, rather than religious, but Australians will react very strongly if they are not allowed to express their disquiet about the source of anti-western sentiments among Muslims, and others who may express such views, in Australia. Amendments in favour of free speech must be explicitly linked to the freedom to express disquiet about Islam in Australia as a source of threat.

The 2016 amendments to discrimination legislation in the ACT, introducing the offence of religious vilification is a sure pointer to the Left's desire to close debate and secure rights for the most illiberal and anti-West religion in Australia, the Muslim religion. The Left will always play the victim card, but they must be out-argued. Invoking security is the Right's card.

Strong obligations for social security to break intergenerational dependence

A Melbourne mother of eight Helen Liumaihetau was quoted in a recent report that "Scott Morrison has his priorities wrong by attacking the culture of welfare dependency in Australia." Liumaihetau had her first daughter when she was 18 and has been out of the workforce since. She remarked, "He should put himself in other people's shoes and live their life for a week and see how things are."[6]

Politicians may find it hard to counter tabloid stories, but the public do not. In response to the tried and true defence of the poor and their advocates, several (of 825) comments on *The Australian* website, replied, "I may as well put myself in your shoes as I probably paid for them." Another, "Perhaps it is time that this woman walked in the shoes of taxpayers." And, "With the amount of tax I pay, I think she has her feet in my shoes." These remarks, in the hundreds, reflect a simple message lost to politicians of the Right, that every dollar spent in the cause of equality is a dollar taken from someone.

The Right has forgotten to argue the case against taking others income to do as the state decides. Every fight for equality, or identity, becomes a further reason to pass a law or take money. One way to fight this attack is to insist that anyone receiving benefits must comply with stringent obligations. Given that 60,000 children, or one in five of all children, are born every year to a woman who is a beneficiary in Australia, and that those children are likely to live on a benefit, it is time that the Right supported the obligation of long-acting reversible contraception for women (male equivalents are not

---

[6] Greg Brown, "Put yourself in my shoes, Scott Morrison, says mother of eight." 26 August 2016 *The Australian.*

available).[7] The New Zealand government has moved to bar women on a benefit from using a subsequent birth of a child to prevent them from returning to, or entering, the workforce. This is a strong and fair message that intervenes in intergenerational dependence when it has the greatest opportunity to change the recipient's behaviour.

More broadly, politicians have created a new dependent constituency through Family Allowances for families where there are at least one and possibly two or more breadwinners. They have created a dependent constituency by subsidised child care to working families, where one partner does not work, that is, is available to care for their children.

The family as an institution has come under fire, often for good reason, but even when the reasons have been good, for example, the impact of women's equality on relationships, governments have intervened and created a dependent constituency in the name of solving the problem. What was the problem? Women controlled their fertility, and women entered the workforce, and shotgun weddings became scarce. These are all good things. Then Australia ends up with the embarrassment of Family Assistance to working families and subsidised childcare to non-working parents.

The last political 'defence of the family' was the Howard government's Baby Bonus, designed to boost the population. It did so, mainly among those least able to care for their children. There should be a conversation, initiated by the Right, about the stance of government when equality of the sexes has been achieved. Many would suggest that point has been reached, for example, there are now more female than male university graduates, so a conversation about the withdrawal of the state subsidies that were meant to ease the outfall from the women's revolution should commence.

---

[7] Gary Johns, 2015. *No Contraception, No Dole: Tackling Intergenerational Welfare Dependence.* Brisbane: Connor Court.

Disbursed power in schooling to break the Left's monopoly on curricula

School funding contains all of the elements that should energise the Right to oppose the status quo. Centralised administration, the commanding heights captured by groups that promote subversive curricula, and over-investment in students who would be more productive and happier in the workforce than in education.

Specifically, the Right has failed parents by funding state schools under a highly centralised system controlled by teachers' unions and education ideologues. Part of the centralisation is the government-to-government relations in the federal system. Because it raises most taxation, the Commonwealth government insists on playing a role in school education. But it transfers money to state governments. It should not do this; it should transfer money to parents.

Parents should receive Commonwealth funds for their child and purchase a position at a school of their choice. One reason is that programs such as 'Safe Schools' and 'climate change' reach a wide population unchallenged; another is that the commanding heights of the school curricula are in the hands of academics and education bureaucrats. The only decent way in which the Right can rest power from this narrow group is by dispersing power to parents, allowing them to choose the school their children should attend and providing a route for them to demand curricula which suit their purposes.

While the Commonwealth does not have constitutional responsibility for the provision of school education, it provides more than $13 billion per year to the states for schools. Commonwealth spending is primarily directed to non-government schools. Spending on government schools is dominated by the states, which provide over 80 per cent of public funding. Implementation of the Gonski 'reforms' would see, however, significant growth in Commonwealth spending on schools over the next decade such that the Commonwealth would no longer be just the primary public funder of non-government schools: it would be a significant funder of government schools' recurrent costs, with the Commonwealth's proportion of contributions projected to increase to around 25 per cent by 2023-24.

The Abbott government's National Commission of Audit recommended the states fund all schools, including the non-government sector. The Commission proposed Commonwealth funding for school education be provided to each state in three pools – one for government schools, one for Catholic systemic schools and one for independent schools. Under this approach, a significant reduction in the size of the Commonwealth Department of Education could be achieved.[8]

This may relieve the size of the Commonwealth bureaucracy but would not drive any change in curricula or efficient teaching. The Commonwealth should hand money to parents so that they can choose the school they wish. They would, over time, drive changes to hiring and firing staff, and also to the curriculum. A major institution would more readily reflect the wishes of the electorate. It is unlikely that the Audit Commission arrangements would do so.

Progress

Australia has reached a point when more people vote for their income than work for it. This is difficult politics for the Right because it too wants to buy votes, but the constituency to which tax cuts appeal has declined and the constituency to which payments appeal has increased.

All governments create constituencies of dependence. It creeps up slowly. For example, all governments thought that they were doing the right thing by taking low-income taxpayers out of the system.

---

[8] National Commission of Audit, 2014. *Towards Responsible Government. Phase One*, 124.

The reasons are varied, but mostly they were because benefits more accurately targeted transfers and tax cuts to the needy. The result, however, was that more citizens made less direct contribution to the pool and no longer associated their 'government' income with the work of others.

There are few libertarian solutions to too much government. The point of politics is to work out how to achieve the destination. The pathway to a liberal society will be multifaceted, part cultural, part regulatory, and designed to win constituencies without bribing them. To achieve a less mutually dependent society, or rather one that is more liberal and governed by contract rather than ideology will take a cultural revolution.

The path to progress, to smaller government, and to liberty will require far-reaching changes. Examples of these might include more stringent conditions on access to benefits; whether assets are tested before receiving the pension; the degree of illness that must be met to qualify for disability payments and an express obligation that you shall not have children while the state is paying for you to re-enter the workforce or to look after existing children. It will take a consumer revolution in school education to break the monopoly of state teachers' unions and bureaucrats, and it will take a fight for free speech so that Australians may feel comfortable debating the level of risk to their security that new entrants pose.

The Provocation of Weakness

Jim Molan

Former senior officer in the Australian Army

Avoiding all conflict should be Australia's highest national interest and a prime objective of Australia's foreign policy. A key tool in avoiding war is deterrence, that is, discouraging an opponent's actions by fear of the consequences. The military plays a key role in deterrence along with all forms of national power and alliances, by raising the cost of aggression.

For Australia's military to be effective it must be capable of deterring conflict but acts of war are often not logical and if deterrence fails, Australia's military must be able to win, to achieve the war aims. That is the standard against which the effectiveness of any military should be judged. That is what is generally referred to in Australia as "Defence" and that is the subject of this Chapter.

Deterrence only works if it is credible. Diplomacy and moral suasion are very important but have more meaning if backed by other forms of power, including military power. In any sort of logical world, there should not be a Right Side of Politics approach to defence and security in Australia, there should only be a realistic approach utilizing all aspects of national power to achieve the national security objectives as decided by the government of the day. If an Australian government wishes to take a course of action involving the use or the threat of the use of force, yet that military force is inadequate for the task, then what China recently said about Australia may be true, we may be a Paper Kitten. If we are, deterrence has failed. Weakness is then provocative.

Is there a Left and Right of defence policy in Australia? In the lead up to the 2013 election I wrote[9]:

> Since Federation, defence policy discussions have generally fallen into two camps: those that focus primarily on Australia's continental geography as the determinant of defence policy, referred to as "Defence of Australia" advocates; and those that focus on Australia's interests in a wider world, popularly referred to as "Expeditionary Operations" advocates.
>
> In general terms, and at a more pronounced level in the period since 1986, a focus on Australia's wider interests in terms of preparing for or conducting operations outside the Australian continent has been a Conservative tradition, while so-called Defence of Australia has been a Labor tradition.
>
> Nothing better explains the failure of defence policy to produce real results than this debate, because both sides of the continental/expeditionary divide are essentially nugatory. If a defence of continental Australia policy was seriously matched by a strategy that was effectively implemented, rather than as a duplicitous means of under-investing in defence, then the force that was produced

[9] Molan Jim, "Why Our Defence Forces face Terminal decline", *Quadrant Magazine*, 1 March 2013

to defend the continent would be more than adequate to conduct any expeditionary operation that any government wanted to conduct.

Australia was able to indulge in this false debate only because there have been no serious consequences for an unrealistic defence policy in Australia up until recently. Our remoteness from centres of conflict, our alliance with the US and no specifically identifiable threats meant that the risk from bad policy was small. All of these have now changed.

There has been a profound shift in the possibility of conflict that impacts on those nations with which Australia is allied, with whom Australia shares values and trade, and which may involve Australia in serious military action.

The disconnect is that this shift towards a higher possibility of conflict is not yet reflected in the capability or readiness of the ADF, despite a solid Defence White Paper in 2016. The full impact of the increase in spending will not be realized for many years, and the spend itself is not linked in an understandable way to how an Australian government may wish to fight, or may be forced to fight.

As the current US Secretary of Defence says, the threat to the world system is four countries and an ideology: Russia, Iran, China, North Korea and Islamic Extremism, not to mention less traditional threats of pandemics, environmental turbulence, cyberspace, space, energy and weapons of mass destruction.

Western intelligence analysts have a bad record in predicting conflicts in the medium or long term, which makes unpredictability the real enemy of defence preparation. This does not mean that there is no threat, it is just that the nature and the source of the threat is non-specific but could arise in a shorter period of time than most western countries would need to prepare for it. This is a difficult concept to sell to Australian voters in a period of hard economic times, when the level of funding of Australian defence is based not on what the ADF may need to defend the nation and its interests, but is based on a view of what the government thinks it can afford.

The result of not linking defence investment tightly to the strategic environment has been chronic underfunding, a policy position that could be rationalized over recent decades but is dangerous now. Before the 2013 election I wrote[10]:

> This underfunding is occurring when no strategist or commentator, national or international, is of the opinion that the strategic environment that Australia faces in our region or world-wide, now or in the next decade or so, is anything but at historically high levels of uncertainty.
>
> In fact the contrary is true. The US is deeply worried. US officials continually stress that emerging Asian powers such as China have benefitted greatly from a rules based system, and it is hoped that this continues. However, double digit rates of building China's armed forces applied over the last 15 years, a legitimate right for any power as long as there is transparency, increases the capability of this emerging power and this must be taken into account when assessing the strategic environment. China's rhetoric would indicate that China does not think of itself as a status quo power but as a revisionist power, and its actions in the South China Sea throughout 2012 have not been rules based, transparent or consistent.

And in recent years the world, with North and South East Asia on the front line, has been trying to manage an even more overtly aggressive China which has managed to prove all its critics right and to successfully frighten all its neighbours. Australia and the world

---

[10] *Ibid*, Molan article.

should welcome the emergence of China as a world power because it immeasurably benefits the Chinese people, the world economy and because China's rise seems inevitable. But we should welcome China's rise from a position of political, military, economic and social strength. If we are not strong in our relationship with China, then our strategy is one of hoping that China treats us well, and hope has never been the basis of good strategy. Our current confusing messages to China as an important trading partner and to the US as our ally need to be reconciled, at least internally.

No one would be a winner out of a war with China therefore every means must be taken to avoid that possibility, most importantly through deterrence. Much comment has resulted from a recent Rand Corporation study[11] of "intense, destructive and protracted" Sino-US war scenarios which would rock the world economy and devastate the region. The study does not predict a Sino-US war but as Professor Paul Dibb[12] says, such a conflict is "plausible (and) … the sort of prudent scenario planning you would expect any military to undertake". The study concludes that the US would be unlikely to lose in the immediate future but in ten years a US victory would be much less certain.

The 2016 Defence White Paper says that "a major conflict between the US and China is unlikely" but this is being challenged as both sides are preparing for conflict, and it would be only prudent to consider the role that Australian defence, especially its military, might play in deterring it or winning it. This is especially so as the ANZUS Treaty commits Australia to 'act to meet the common danger in accordance with its constitutional processes'. It is impossible to accurately predict how such a conflict could eventuate, how it

[11] Gompert, David C., Astrid Cevallos and Cristina L. Garafola. War with China: Thinking Through the Unthinkable. Santa Monica, CA: RAND Corporation, 2016. http://www.rand.org/pubs/research_reports/RR1140.html. Also available in print form.
[12] Brendan Nicholson, "Warning of 'intense' war as China's military might approaches US", *The Australian,* 15 August 2016.

would run and how it might be terminated. A less sanguine view than RAND[13] is that "...it is entirely possible that in a lengthy high-intensity conflict (between US and China), economic losses would be equivalent, decisive military engagements would be elusive, and China's post-war recovery would be faster. Combined with the benefit of regional proximity and a weakened allied presence in the Western Pacific, this means the possibility of a Chinese strategic victory in 2025 or beyond cannot be excluded".

At the same time as China's rise, there has been a significant deterioration in comparative US military power. This is due to the demands of current wars, war weariness within US society, a less assertive US political leadership on international affairs, and an overall reduction in spending on defence resulting in a definite reduction in force levels even accounting for the end of the large deployments to Iraq and Afghanistan, and in readiness compared to the tasks that need to be addressed.[14]

If the US has doubts about its ability to deal militarily with either China or Russia by themselves, then coordinated or opportunistic action by a combination of revisionist or rogue nations should be of the deepest concern to Australian governments. Should there be

---

[13] This discussion was played out recently in *Michael O'Hanlon and David Petraeus* "America's Awesome Military And How to Make It Even Better", Foreign Affairs, Sep/Oct 2016, and Justin Johnson "The Military's Real Readiness Crisis; Petraeus & O'Hanlon Are Wrong", Breaking Defence, 17 August 2016.

[14] Top US military leaders speak of "Carter-era" readiness problems and a hollow military. While many of the details are classified, statements by military leaders indicating that US readiness is at "historically low levels", is "widespread", there are "grave concerns about the readiness of our forces" to deal with Russia or China, today's defense budget is "well below the minimums agreed to by bipartisan experts", only "one-third of this historically small force are considered ready for high-end combat", "less than half of all Air Force squadrons are ready for combat and there are serious shortages of both pilots and mechanics", and "pilot flying hours (i.e. training) have fallen dramatically". Even those less critical say that the US military is certainly "neither broken nor unready for combat, but its size and resource levels are less than is advisable given the range of contemporary threats and the missions for which it has to prepare", and "the navy's fleet and the army are too small, and current budget trajectories imply further cuts rather than increases".

a need to deploy US forces to a significant NATO or Middle East contingency, then there may not be much left for our region. The military pivot to the Pacific, despite the rhetoric, has to date "been relatively modest in scale, with a net shifting of assets to the Asia-Pacific theater of no more than $10 billion to $15 billion worth out of the approximately $600 billion annual defense budget, by our estimates", and with an attitude in the US military that "no 'pivot' to the Pacific is needed or even truly possible given the United States' other interests and commitments".[15]

There is an expectation in the US that Australia should be able to look after its own backyard and that we are the experts in this Region, but can we do that with the ADF at its current levels and given the current spending plans? This is what needs to be addressed and addressed publicly. Even if the US wanted to assist Australia in a military contingency, there may not be enough US Cavalry to come to anyone's rescue. Australia suffered in the last world war from its allies prioritizing Europe and the Middle East over the Pacific.

Australian voters assume that defence is being handled adequately because governments spend what to voters are large amounts on defence. Most of the Australian population are at best vaguely aware of the increase in threat levels across the world, and the reduction in the comparative dominance of the US. An element in the Australian population even holds the view that Australia is not defendable, and these people question all levels of defence expenditure. One may forgive an ordinary Australian for holding such views, but there is no excuse for analysts or strategist to apparently be so remiss, or for governments to not insist that the dots be joined and to show leadership on defence. Australia's potential opponents will know our defence capability far more accurately than most members of the Government and most voters.

---

[15] *Op Cit*, Breaking Defence.

No Australian political party has a deeply held defence philosophy. All have defence policies which specify only inputs to defence (ships, planes, tanks, people etc) but do not address meaningfully the output of defence (the ability to defend this country against certain threats of a certain nature in a certain period of time, as well as providing forces for lesser contingencies) and so achieve deterrence. Without a deeply held defence philosophy based on an assessment of both the security environment and the true capability of the ADF, how can a party in government know it is meeting the needs of the nation?

There is a tendency for the Australian government to value Defence more for its innovation, technology and job creation capability, rather than as a means to defend Australia across the full spectrum of threats. Defence planning is therefore based only on a perception of what can be afforded, rather than what is needed, which goes against creating a joint modern balanced force. If political leaders and voters concentrate only on what is considered affordable and not on what is needed, then all will feel satisfied on defence issues if governments merely achieve their own stated expenditure goals; they will not question whether the expenditure goals themselves are appropriate.

The result is that for decades, the planning process for defence has been grossly distorted in that it does not initially specify the force that is needed to match a realistic threat and so produce a certain acceptable level of risk. A defence planning process with integrity should initially specify the required force without resource constraints, and having done that, only then should governments apply the funding constraint that they are prepared to spend. We pay governments to take risks on issues such as defence, but only by adopting a defence planning process that has integrity and some transparency for voters. It is critically important to specify the risk that a government is taking at various levels of expenditure to achieve certain outputs. That way, governments themselves know what risks they are taking, and voters can judge what governments are doing in their name. Defence is trying to create the internal mechanism to do this, but governments must own the process and the result.

The consequence of the current strategic environment is that the traditional role of the ADF to provide small, tailored, single service forces for limited periods for counter insurgency and/or counter terrorism distant from Australia, now needs to be supplemented by an ability to generate joint sophisticated warfighting forces of increased scale and readiness.

The Defence White Paper 2016 is the best in the series of Defence White Papers since the first one in 1976, but the threat environment has changed not just since 1976, but most dramatically over the long period of gestation of the White Paper itself. The investment made in defence is impressive in dollar terms, and especially so when compared to the neglect of the Labor governments that produced the 2009 and 2013 White Papers. But the force that should emerge to defend Australia over the coming decade as a result of this policy is the force that we should have right now, given the strategic environment we now face. Such a force would give us a credible medium level hedging strategy, and we should now be considering what changes we may need to implement in the future, in the face of a more combative Asia, and a more combative world. Australia's defence is seriously out of sync with the world as it is. Despite the 2016 Defence White Paper, we are five to fifteen years behind.

In a doctrinal sense, the hard power component of deterrence strategy (the ADF) has two key requirements; a credible force-in-being and capacity for competitive mobilisation. A credible force-in-being must be able to manage the strategic environment, to decrease the incidence of conflict and when unavoidable to gain sufficient time to mobilise the means to defeat specific threats to the nation. Competitive mobilisation is the capability to turn the latent potential of the nation into fighting power and requires investment not only in the Defence industry, but in education, energy security and a feasible strategy of mobilisation. A credible force-in-being and capacity for competitive mobilisation requires statesmen who weigh the consequences of not only short term political and policy risk, but long term strategic risk.

It is important to acknowledge that the ADF, as a fighting force, is better than it has been probably since the end of the Vietnam War. This is thanks to decisions made during the Howard government, decisions of the Abbott and Turnbull governments, continual exposure of the ADF to operations, and solid military leadership and advocacy to government. The Air Force that good conservative government policy has produced is world class, although its capability for sustained combat in defence of the nation is questioned. The Navy is solving many of the problems that lack of funding has created, in particular with submarine availability, and is starting to see the vessels produced as a result of conservative government policy enter service, though the majority will not do so for years if not decades, in part due to Labor procrastination on defence. The Army has the best combat experience for many years but runs the risk of being seen to be of a lower priority than the other Services. This reflects an illogical, bureaucratic strategic thought process which is mind boggling in its stupidity, and which works against the ADF being able to fight successfully in a modern conflict, which the military call being 'Joint'. Once again we see signs of hollowing out of army units and a lack of readiness. So there is much that is good in where the ADF is now, but Australians have a right to know if the ADF is good enough for the current and perhaps much worse future strategic environment. Despite tactical competence in recent wars, we still do not know what the ADF is really good at, and we do not know where our fracture points are.

Because of the neglect of the ADF during the six years of the recent Labor government, commentators were thankful that a target of 2% of GDP to be spent on Defence within a decade was adopted by the Abbott government. But how much is enough and what do we get for our money? I addressed this in some detail in 2012, assuming that the strategic environment would remain about the same:[16]

> We were able to see what close to 2% of GDP could have been able to produce in terms of capability, because that was what came out of the Howard years, but was overturned by PM Rudd before it could overcome decades of neglect. We can see what can be produced for 1.8% of GDP, because that is the marginal defence force and defence industry that we have now (2012). We are about to see what 1.6% of GDP produces because that is the level of defence funding that the Government has now approved (2013) and that, as it bites, will produce a defence force in terminal decline. We are likely to see what 1.4% of GDP produces which is what the future holds for the ADF according to the budget papers (forward estimates). At a sustained level of 1.4% funding, the ADF will be fixed in its terminal decline, and even if resources were suddenly found, would require years if not decades to bring real military capability back to the ADF. Finally, we can see, by looking across the Tasman, the military impotence that is created by 1% of GDP, the current level of defence expenditure in NZ.
>
> The magic number that produces usable military capability for Australia in the strategic environment in 2012 is about 2% of GDP. **But that amount needs to be spent over years or even decades to produce an appropriate defence effect.** What 2% of GDP produces is described by ASPI as a "medium level hedging strategy for the ADF".

---

[16] Op Cit, *Quadrant.*

This means that it produces an ADF that looks like Force 2030 (the force that came out of the 2009 Defence White Paper) and that can conduct a level of sophisticated joint warfighting operations appropriate to a nation such as Australia. It is a level of defence investment where most systems that exist in the ADF actually work, where they could be taken up to their highest (and most expensive) level of operational capability in a reasonable period of time (for most in about six months), which serves as a basis for expansion if the strategic environment goes seriously bad, and gives government real options for the use of military force. 2% does not defend Australia or its interests against a major Asian power. To spend less than 2% in this strategic environment, and the Labor Government is proposing that significantly less than 2% be spent, would undermine Australia's strategic credibility in our region, and therefore undermine the security of our region.

A 2% spend on defence after a few years would give Australia confidence that it possessed a force capable of reinforcing the integrated system of strategic deterrence that inhibits early resort to force by any regional player. As such, the current strategy of hoping that nothing bad will happen could be abandoned.

If the strategic situation became even less predictable then, for example, another 0.5% of GDP might be needed. The dynamic is that once you have been at 2% for several years, expansion in the worst case to higher level of expenditure is made infinitely more possible. To go from Labor's 1.5% to a force that needed 3% of GDP in a reasonable period of time would be almost impossible, regardless of the availability of funding. The Rudd/Gillard Governments seem not to have learnt from the old saying: "In peacetime you have lots of time and no money, in wartime you have lots of money and no time". Defence expenditure is all about risk, but 1.5% of GDP spent on defence is not a mature assessment of risk, it is irresponsibility.

Levels of expenditure around 2% are appropriate when Australia does not face a direct threat, but if we were faced with what ASPI calls a "combative Asia", exhibiting a tendency towards conflict, Australia may find that it has to spend as much as 3 or 4% of GDP. This is high by recent Australian standards, but would be acceptable to the Australian people because the reason behind the increased spend would be very obvious to every Australian.

This 2% expenditure goal looks like being reached three years earlier than promised by PM Abbott, not necessarily because of any increased government commitment, but due to the impact of foreign exchange supplementation caused by the depreciation of the Australian dollar and falling GDP growth projections. The illogicality of meeting a fixed percentage target because of GDP projections having fallen should be apparent to all.[17] But an even greater threat to defence capability is the present economic state of the nation, the weakness of the parliamentary position of recent Australian governments, the lack of focus on the likelihood of war, and a serious lack of process in formulating strategy in government and in the bureaucracy, especially the relationship between when the nation acknowledges that there is a threat (Defence Warning Time) and when expansion or mobilization begins (Defence Preparation Time). Expansion and mobilisation will rarely be facilitated by an opponent's actions until far too late. In the absence of imminent threat, reliance on national myths such as dependence on allies or

---

[17] ASPI, "The Cost of Defence. ASPI Defence Budget Brief 2016-17", May 2016, p. vii.

the natural Australian soldier, run the risk of collapsing mid-conflict when what is promised or assumed fails to become reality.

Therefore the profound shift in the threat environment means that the traditional role of the ADF, to provide small forces for wars of choice distant from Australia, now needs to be supplemented by serious preparations for the conduct of high end joint warfighting in defence of the nation. Work has commenced on this in Defence but it should not be driven by the Army, the Navy, the Air Force or Defence, but owned, understood and driven by an output focussed conservative government with a defence philosophy.

As a nation with the fifth highest per capita income, the twelfth highest GDP and the fifty-fourth highest population of about 200 countries in the world, the only thing that Australia needs to defend itself, even against extreme threats, is resolve and time. The more resolve we develop now, the less time we will need in the future, and the greater our ability to deter conflict or to win if deterrence fails.

The ABCs of a Conservative's Anger at the Liberal Party

Roger Franklin

Online Editor of *Quadrant*

Late one evening toward the end of August, 2016, after a galling day and in no mood to put up with further irritation, I turned on the telly to be confronted by the alarming spectacle of two young and naked men copulating with each other and, simultaneously, a chimpanzee. The ABC's costumers – it was an ABC show, of course it was – had done a fine job with the chimp, for it took a long and hard second look to be assured it was actually some small sort of person suited-up in simian drag. What they were up to atop a rock in the bush – not to mention in the corner of my living room – was immediately evident from the tangle of limbs, all hairy to one degree or another and writhing in a ball of ostentatious carnal intent. That it was a scene from a comedy production was somewhat harder to discern, as fusty tradition endorses the notion that alleged vehicles for wit and mirth should prompt at least a grin, perhaps even the odd giggle. What became apparent as further scenes unfolded was that humour in and of itself could never have been the scriptwriters' intent. This particular programme, a hip-dude local production billed as *Soul Mates*, sought to shock and nothing more. The skits were jarring, crass and pointlessly so, cartoonishly surreal and, of course, larded with random obscenities because, once again, this was an ABC production. The very idea that it was being broadcast at all, let alone underwritten by Australia's taxpayers, well that must have been the joke – if a slap to the face can ever be described as a joke.

And a slap it was, delivered from a position of arrogant, unassailable authority. Free from fear and possibility of being called to account, someone at the national broadcaster had made the risk-free decision to put *Soul Mates* on the production schedule. Someone must have thought there was a point to it. But as the show eschewed humour in any recognised form, what could possibly have been perceived as its worth? Why, you can almost hear the pitch:

> *"And we'll have these naked gay guys in a menage a trois with a monkey. How 'bout that!"*

> *"Wow! That will shock the squares."*

Normally at such moments, weary from a day's work at *Quadrant Online*, which it is my privilege to edit, and confronted yet again by another of the ABC's innovative interpretations of the "quality programming" its Charter demands, the reaction to such a spectacle would be to roll the eyes and reach for the channel-changer, all the while wondering yet again why a government-run, but decidedly unsupervised, broadcaster is needed at all. A broad sampling of alternate fare scrolled past as the screen surfed through terrestrial and cable offerings, and there was NetFlix as well if I could have been bothered hooking up the computer. On any other night it would have been a cinch to find something diverting on an alternate station or network, and so it might have been on that evening also. But it had been a vexing few days, as I said, with circumstances conspiring to produce a prickly dyspepsia in regard to, well, pretty much everything.

Two chaps and their love-slave chimp brought that amorphous disquiet suddenly into the sharpest focus. With something akin to a masochist's perverse delight in being insulted and demeaned, I returned to *Soul Mates*.

Neither clever nor funny and most definitely not in accord with its Charter, how had the ABC come to air this sophomoric assault on good taste? The answer is simple: because it could do so without fear of recrimination and with utter disregard for the inevitable objections. Not so long ago another alleged comedy show depicted a conservative columnist in *flagrante delicto* with a dog. No one was fired, despite the incident resulting in a belated apology and substantial pay-out; indeed the program's producers have kept right on landing contracts to churn out more of the only slightly less offensive same. Chimp-buggering and dog-bothering – this is what we get, I thought, after decades of ceding our public institutions and instrumentalities to a small, tight class consisting entirely of the insistently and incestuously self-pleasuring. We pay, they play – and don't for as moment kid yourself that the slightest attention will ever be paid to public outrage, no matter how heated or widespread.

At that moment disgust took charge – disgust with the ABC certainly, but more than that, disgust with conservatives for our supine acceptance of the left's control of budgets, culture and the public pulpit.

And it isn't just the ABC. We grumble and tell each other how wicked it is that a race commissioner calls for public complaints in order to harass a newspaper cartoonist who has dared to address a theme he would prefer to see left unexplored, but we do nothing to demand reform or, better yet, to scuttle the Human Rights Commission's crew of business-class jet-abouts. And sure, we notice TV ads depicting domestic violence as the sole province of white men and boys, and we share the truth amongst ourselves that if you lay the census maps charting Indigenous populations on top of those for regional crime, the overlap would make it impossible not to conclude that domestic violence is overwhelmingly an Aboriginal vice. Yet we do nothing (except mutter and grumble) while the producers of such ads feather their nests with the next grant, the next production contract, the next job lot of appointments for mates and mentors.

Let me further explain my anger on that Night of the Amorous Ape by re-winding to the previous day's beginning, when the radio by my bed came to life at 7am with the sound of an ABC voice interviewing one of the interchangeable Trades Hall apparatchiks who have coagulated in the grease trap that is Victorian Premier Daniel Andrews' cabinet. Great things were about to be done for the environment, apparently, as the Andrews' government was re-asserting its election pledge to shut down a coal-burning electricity plant in the LaTrobe Valley. Renewables were the way to go, the Labor voice assured its interlocutor, adding it would be a terrible pity if Victoria allowed South Australia to corner all those green jobs and international kudos which wind turbines and the like are said to bestow. A few weeks later, of course, South Australia would go black as a direct consequence of all that green goodness, but on this morning it was the interviewer's obsequious feting of "sustainable" nostrums which rankled. The plant nominated for closure produced better than 20% of Victoria's energy. What sort of a government crimps the supply of power to industry and individual homes? More to the point, what sort of journalist neglects to raise such a key question with his or her subject?

The habit of journalists to conduct interviews from bended knee is a particular bugbear of mine, as there was a time, and not so long ago, when journalism was supposed to be the province of the perpetual outsider. Comfort the afflicted and afflict the comfortable, that sort of thing. The idea drummed into me as a cub reporter was that one was obliged to honour that instruction regardless of personal sympathy and conviction. Today's newsrooms? Well just look at the garrulous children who inhabit them.

At the local coffee shop over breakfast, I picked up *The Age* and glanced through the thin offerings of a dying, palsied rag. Women's issues … green issues … the odium of Tony Abbott and malevolence of Donald Trump – these weren't news stories, I thought, so much as the passions of the Twitterverse reproduced in the increasingly obsolescent medium of dead trees and ink. Worse than that, where there was an actual news "hook" to a story, it had been made the excuse for a sermon. Or consider this: Tony Abbott wins an election, as he did in 2013, and an *Age* columnist, Clementine Ford, immediately launches a range of 'Fuck Abbott' T-shirts; worse, the paper and its related websites promote her enterprise and obscenity by awarding online links to the site where the garments might be purchased. According to Fairfax Media's chairman, the *Age* will likely soon cease publication, the *Sydney Morning Herald* too. It must never occur to him that habitually and gratuitously alienating 50% of your potential market is not a good survival strategy. Still, it works for some. The executive in question gets around in a Maserati.

I tossed the wretched travesty of a newspaper aside, no better informed and with irritation mounting, and proceeded to Altonagate, my local shopping mall, entertained (for want of a better word) in the car by Radio National. The tail end of one item suggested that, yet again, those who shape the news were under the impression that listening taxpayers needed to be reminded how our planet is at the very brink of environmental and ecological collapse. Some ardent professor of glib greenery was being quoted at length about the catastrophe to come unless we "do something" about farting cows or disaffected coral polyps or, come to think of it, Victorians' access to ready and reliable electricity.

Call me a cynic, but I suspected the special "something" the speaker most desired to be a swag of larger ARC grants that would underwrite his mortgage, further career and further soliciting of yet more ARC funding. The windscreen wipers slashed against a driving rain as I drove, and the temperature outside was in the single digits. It was, in other words, a morning entirely representative of what had been a shockingly cold and thoroughly miserable winter, even by Melbourne's capricious yardstick. But in that ABC studio the curse of sweaty carbon ruled unchallenged. We listeners in our scarves and raincoats would just have to accept that the world is not as we see and experience it – at that moment miserable, wet and cold – but as we are informed by our grant-fed catastropharian betters. They were quoting Tim Flannery when it became a choice between nausea and another station. The pre-set button on my car's stereo won that contest.

Alas, no comfort elsewhere on the AM band. The local ABC outlet was blabbering and blubbering about how wonderful it is that our formerly sterile society had been culturally enriched by the wholesale importation of – what do they call it? – ah, yes, that's right, *otherness*. Later that week such wonderful diversity would be celebrated, as it is every Friday, by a special clinic at the Royal Women's Hospital for victims of female genital mutilation. Funny thing how only certain aspects of multiculturalism seem to rate the attention of the authorised, officially approved media.

There was more multiculturalism to be observed inside the mall, and the spectacle did nothing to placate the day's irritations. Strolling along in Western attire was a bearded gent who matched what the police are given to describing as being of "Middle Eastern appearance". Behind him shuffled a burka's black sack of a creature, a woman presumably, and behind her came two young girls who could have been no older than eleven, yet each had already been consigned to a lifetime of hijabbery. At the very back came a bouncing moppet with hair still free. Her future imprisonment in the prescribed garments of a genuinely misogynistic patriarchy was, quite literally, just ahead of her. For a brief moment there was a strong urge to tap the black sack on what I presumed to be its shoulder and advise that, this being Australia, she didn't have to dress that way, that no man, culture or creed has the right to deny her the touch of sun on skin, the liberty to be seen as a person rather than a possession wrapped in a bolt of black.

I bit my tongue, however. The *Australian*'s cartoonist, Bill Leak, was just then being smeared as a racist for depicting three Aborigines – a policeman, a miscreant youngster and his drunken father – in a pointed illustration of a truth few but he dare to utter, at least openly: that Indigenous miseries have much less to do with the legacy of disease-ridden blankets and poisoned flour than grog and appalling parenting. There was even a petition doing the rounds in media circles and, to their eternal shame, professed journalists were adding their names, Fairfax and ABC worthies prominent amongst them; likewise, numerous journalism academics from our universities. How did Australia's newsrooms come to be infested with social justice warriors? If you can no longer bring yourself to read the politically correct and ideologically sound publications for which they work, blame a teacher.

That night it was dinner with my elderly mother, who enjoys the roasts at the local RSL club and a flutter on the pokies. She was happy to get out and about, but the evening only made my irritation that much worse. While waiting for her lemon squash and my rough red to be poured, I noticed the mirror behind the bar had been papered with warnings about, well, everything to do with the perils of pleasure. As I wasn't pregnant, I could ignore the poster advising never to take a drink. The one grimly referencing the ills of tobacco was somewhat harder to ignore, likewise the much repeated advice that alcohol would affect my driving, liver and temper – the last message delivered by the image of a battered woman. For good measure, the cavalcade of admonitions advised me to be wary of gambling too much and – the one sign of any genuine worth – not to spew salty language, presumably after blowing my pay-cheque on Queen of the Nile or, angry and in my cups after ignoring the other admonitions against excess, overcome by the yen to give some blameless woman a thorough thumping.

Mum, who has been around for some 90 years, accepted her lemon squash with ladylike grace and agreed that, all things considered, the Australia she knew and loved was gone. She even had a theory to explain its demise. "Life is safe these days," she said, "too safe in some ways." It was an interesting take on the endemic nanny-ism and ubiquitous, state-sanctioned hectoring. In her youth she had seen the Great Depression and grew to so hate the taste of rabbit, the meat of the poor, she will not touch it even now. Then came the war and the boys she had known from school who did not come home. Polio eliminated, TB all but vanquished, antibiotics, life-lengthening surgeries and technologies … it once was believed, as Mum noted between sips, that anyone who chalked up a healthy three score and ten had won life's lottery, done pretty well for themselves. Now, rather than a blessing, 70 safe years are seen as an entitlement, with any twist of fate or circumstance subtracting from that number regarded as something it is the job of elected representatives to remedy with the assistance of lecturing public broadcasters, with laws and fines and punitive taxes. All that, and just to remind us that adults are no better than overgrown children, broad acres of killjoy signage on every barman's wall.

Mum's is a good theory, probably right as well, but it doesn't address the half of it, the half that really matters. That would be the simple fact that the orthodoxy of contemporary comportment and belief is wholly that of the left. No one pushes back, not on the airwaves or in the streets, not in the courts or in our parliaments, where the leading conservative party is also of the left, just a tad less so. Consider Victoria as the perfect example of a "conservative" government that wasn't, not by a long chalk.

Begin with the matter of ideology – a dirty word, it seems, during the Baillieu/Napthine government which, much to its surprise, came to office in 2010, survived but a single term and was largely indistinguishable from the Labor administration which preceded it. Against logic, it funded its enemies, as when Baillieu, only then just settling into the premier's office, shared an affable table with a gaggle of luvvies at the state's Literary Awards. They took the grants that flowed from Spring Street – then went right back to laughing at their benefactors. Did anyone in the private councils of Baillieu's government suggest that it might be a good idea to clean out the arts collective, rather than feeding it the mother's milk of taxpayer funds? If they did, one gathers they were told to shut up, that such a move could only inspire black-clad legions of the artistic and angry to converge on the parliament's steps and say rude things about Liberals.

Meanwhile, the conservative faithful waited in vain. When Vice Squad cops raided a taxpayer-funded St Kilda gallery and carted away "art" that featured pictures of apple-cheeked lads with monstrous erections, some of us hoped the responsible minister would withdraw support or, at the very least, wonder aloud why the public purse should be underwriting industrial strength obscenity.

Instead, silence.

Somewhere, standing by a machine or sitting at a workaday desk, a Victorian resident was paying the taxes that hung such filth on the gallery's wall. He or she might not even have known of the police raid, but a minister standing up for genuine art, not to mention good taste, would have made headlines and an impression, perhaps even won some votes. But not a peep of rebuke from the then-government's benches was forthcoming and the grants never stopped flowing.

When given the chance the electorate decided in 2014 that there was no difference between the parties and opted for the flashier alternative. That silence, that cowardice if you will, is once again conspicuous, this time in Canberra. As I type I wait in vain for Prime Minister Malcolm Turnbull to utter the words '*je suis* Bill Leak'. But no, there is only silence and betrayal, not merely of free speech but also of conservative voters' reasonable expectations when they placed their first preference beside the name of a Coalition candidate.

Where is the cry that Australia's bloated, bureaucrat-beset tertiary institutions need desperately to be reformed? Degrees in lesbian calligraphy are all very well, but an emphasis on hard science would be of more use, and do more good, for the nation's future. Certainly we could get by with fewer journalism graduates.

The galloping passivity of conservatives, elected and otherwise, it galls and appals. At *Quadrant Online*, for example, I must regularly spike essays I would dearly like to publish for fear of writs and "lawfare". Yes, we'd likely win those battles, but the cost of fighting them would be to lose in and of itself. Are there no conservative lawyers out there, lawyers who believe in freedom of speech and are prepared to back their convictions with a few pro bono hours? For more than two decades I lived and worked in the United States, where conservatives fight back when pushed. There are think tanks and institutions aplenty dedicated to free minds and free markets – Hudson, Cato, Claremont, Hoover – funded by benefactors and dedicated to the proposition that, unless the left is challenged and confronted at every turn, there is no hope of halting the long march of its acolytes, the machinations of its social engineers.

Perhaps it is too late in Australia, where so much ground has been surrendered and there remains precious little left to defend. Our alleged conservative champions are playing of us for suckers, folks. If they weren't, well let's just say that Bill Leak could draw his cartoons without keeping an attorney's business card handy. As to evening viewing, we would see fewer fornicating chimps on the ABC.

Classical Liberalism, the Australian media and the ghost of Governor Darling

Rebecca Weisser

Rebecca Weisser is a journalist, editor and public policy and communications consultant.

Australia has been a pioneer of political liberalism. Unfortunately, illiberalism also has a deep well-spring. The interaction of these two forces, over more than a century, has resulted in Australian media laws that are anachronistic and oppressive and require urgent attention particularly regarding freedom of expression, protection of property rights, media ownership and public broadcasting.

Freedom of expression

From the earliest days of British settlement through to the 21st century, governments have attempted to muzzle the media. These attempts – from Governor Darling to Prime Minister Julia Gillard and Senator Bob Brown – were driven by anger at the way the press reported on the government.

The colony's first newspapers were subjected to government censorship.[1] When it was lifted in 1824, it was not long before Governor Ralph Darling wanted to silence his critics by licensing papers and imposing a stamp duty.[2] He argued this was necessary for the security of the colony because newspapers were stirring up discontent[2] but Chief justice, (Sir) Francis Forbes, refused writing:

> ...every free man has the right of using the common trade of printing and publishing newspapers; by the proposed bill this right is confined to such persons only as the Governor may deem proper. By the laws of England, the liberty of the press is regarded as a constitution privilege, which liberty consists in exemption from previous restraint – by the proposed bill a preliminary licence is required which is to destroy the freedom of the press and to place it at the discretion of the Government.

Unfortunately, the rest of Darling's Act became law, compelling publishers to lodge 300 pounds to ensure they could pay libel fines and empowering the courts to banish a person from the colony for a second offence.[3] Publishers were sent to prison or heavily fined.[4] Happily, a change of government in Britain brought a new under-secretary of state who rebuked Darling for trying to suppress free speech.[5]

---

[1] Pressreference.com, http://www.pressreference.com/A-Be/Australia.html

[2] Sir Ralph Darling, *Australian Dictionary of Biography*, Volume 1, MUP, 1966.

[2] Jolly, Rhonda & Australia. Parliamentary Library (issuing body) 2016, Media ownership and regulation: a chronology. Part one. from print to radio days and television nights, Canberra Parliamentary Library. (http://trove.nla.gov.au/work/2046119950).

[3] Ibid.

[4] Ibid.

[5] Ibid.

Sacred vigilantes and secular speech police

Nothing better encapsulates contemporary threats to the Australian media than the plight of *The Australian*'s cartoonist, Bill Leak. Bloodthirsty jihadists and political correctness crusaders are united in the cause of silencing him. Their means differ but not their ends. "They're both in the shut-up business."[6] They both claim a monopoly on truth.

Each draws authority from a legal text. Jihadists invoke Sharia Law, which, according to them, gives them the right to murder anyone who mocks the Prophet. Leak finds himself condemned by verses 33:57 and 33:61 of the Koran: "Lo! Those who malign Allah and his messenger … Accursed, they will be seized wherever found and slain with a (fierce) slaughter."[7]

The political correctness crusaders invoke Section 18C of the 1975 Racial Discrimination Act (RDA),[8] which makes it unlawful to "offend, insult, humiliate or intimidate another person or group of people … because of the race, colour or national or ethnic origin of the other person or of some or all of the people in the group." Section 18D of the same act theoretically exempts "anything said or done reasonably and in good faith … in making or publishing … a fair comment on any event or matter of public interest if the comment is an expression of a genuine belief held by the person making the comment."

What constitutes "fair comment", however, or the "expression of a genuine belief" is in the eyes of the beholder, as the trial of columnist Andrew Bolt demonstrated. Justice Mordecai Bromberg found that Bolt had not written 'reasonably and in good faith' because

---

[6] Mark Steyn, Complications and Curating, The War on Free Speech, steynonline.com, 17 October 2016

[7] What does Islam Teach about … Killing Critics, thereligionofpeace.com, http://www.thereligionofpeace.com/pages/quran/insulters-islam.aspx

[8] http://www.comlaw.gov.au/ComLaw/Legislation/ActCompilation1.nsf/0/29DCCB9 139D4CCD8CA256F71004E4063/$file/RDA1975.pdf

"insufficient care and diligence was taken to minimise the offence, insult, humiliation and intimidation suffered by the people likely to be affected..." In particular, the judge said Bolt should not be exempt because of his articles' "derisive tone, the provocative and inflammatory language and the inclusion of gratuitous asides."

"I didn't know satire was a crime yet,"[9] Bolt pleaded at his trial. Now we do. He might have added, as Juvenal did in the 1st century AD, "In times like these it is difficult not to write satire."[10]

Justice Bromberg wrapped up his 57,000-word judgment claiming that "it is important that nothing in the order I make should suggest that it is unlawful for a publication to deal with racial identification, including by challenging the genuineness of the identification of a group of people."

Yet there can be little doubt that Bolt's trial had a chilling effect on writers and editors. The legal action dragged on for a year, at a cost of hundreds of thousands of dollars to Bolt's publisher, News Corp Australia. The punishment was more than the cost, however, it was the gruelling court process and the innuendo -- gratuitous asides if you prefer – falsely linking Bolt's articles to eugenics, the Nuremberg Race Laws and Holocaust denial.

Finkelstein's News Media Council

The ambit of the Racial Discrimination Act however was clearly too limited for those who wanted to restrict more generally what is said in the press. On 14 September 2011, the Gillard government appointed Justice Ray Finkelstein to head an Independent Media Inquiry. Ostensibly, it was called because of phone hacking at the *News of the World* in the UK, which led the British government to set

---

[9] Michael O'Connor, Andrew Bolt on Trial, *Quadrant Online,* 1 May 2011
[10] Satire I, Line 30.

up the Leveson Inquiry in July 2011 into the culture, practices and ethics of the British press.[11] In fact, as former editor-in-chief of *The Age* Michael Gawenda wrote, it "was a politically motivated inquiry set up by a government urged on by its Greens partners that didn't like the way some sections of the media, the News Limited papers in particular, were covering politics."[12]

The report, delivered on 28 February 2012, was a sinister document, underpinned by a disturbing belief in the role of government in subsidising approved private sector media[13] and woefully out of touch. Finkelstein called for websites with as few as "15,000 hits per annum" to be regulated by the News Media Council,"[14] about as sensible as trying to regulate telephone conference calls and group email.[15] The report said there was little evidence of "a wholesale shift of classified advertising from newspapers to the Internet;[16] online advertising was merely creating "pressure point in the industry,"[17] calling to mind the Monty Python scene where the Black Knight suffers a series of "pressure-point creation incidents", said one industry executive, adding, "Finkelstein and his advisors simply don't understand online media…"[18]

But all this pales beside Finkelstein's extraordinary recommendation to create an all-powerful, unaccountable, government-funded News

[11] Brian Leveson (November 2012). *An Inquiry Into the Culture, Practices and Ethics of the Press (Volume 1)*

[12] Michael Gawenda, *The Australian*, 5 March 2013

[13] Report of the Independent Inquiry into the Media and Media Regulation, R. Finkelstein assisted by M Ricketson, 28 February 2012, P. 331 12.88 - P. 333 12.97 and P. 290_ 11.44 – P. 300 11.86.

[14] Ibid.

[15] David Walker, WorkDay Media, http://shorewalker.com/policy/the-finkelstein-reviews-fatal-flaws.html

[16] Report of the Independent Inquiry into the Media and Media Regulation, R. Finkelstein assisted by M Ricketson, 28 February 2012, p.83, 3.63.

[17] Ibid, p.18, 1.18.

[18] David Walker, WorkDay Media, http://shorewalker.com/policy/the-finkelstein-reviews-fatal-flaws.html

Media Council to make the news media "more accountable to those covered in the news, and to the public generally."[19] It would "set journalistic standards for the news media ... and handle complaints made by the public ..."[20] It could also initiate investigations off its own bat. It would have the "power to require a news media outlet to publish an apology, correction or retraction, or afford a person a right to reply" and its decisions would be "binding" – "any failure to comply with the court order should be contempt of court and punishable in the usual way".[21]

There would be no internal appeal and no external review via the Administrative Appeals Tribunal.[22] Only in the course of enforcement proceedings might a challenge to a determination be available but this, apparently, "would provide sufficient mechanism for judicial supervision."[23]

The 20 members of the Council would include three senior academics (appointed by the Australian Vice-Chancellor's committee), the Commonwealth Ombudsman and the Solicitor-General and of the rest, half would be members of the public, the other half would be nominated by the media and the media union but managers, directors and shareholders of media organisations could not be nominated.

The report was "suffused with a sort of academic elitism,"[24] which tried to gloss over the fact that a kangaroo court would act as lawmaker and judge, beyond the reach of parliament, with the power to tell editors how and what to run in their papers, and to fine them or send them or their journalists to prison if they didn't

---

[19] Ibid.
[20] Ibid.
[21] Ibid.
[22] Ibid. P. 299 11.78
[23] Ibid. P. 299 11.79
[24] Michael Gawenda, *The Australian*, 5 March 2013

comply. Governor Darling would have been delighted.

Jonathan Holmes, former host of ABC1's *Media Watch* wrote, "I think Mr. Finkelstein's own report demonstrates why the notion that a panel of worthies should sit in judgment over the news media, backed by the force of law, is ... 'absolutely alarming'."[25]

Diversity of ownership

The Gillard government's motives had many precedents. The Labor Party has long been suspicious of privately-owned media. In the days before wireless telegraphy, it wanted its own newspaper in each capital – a dream it didn't fulfil although it did set up some papers including the *Labor Daily* which was published in Sydney in between 1922 and 1941.[26]

The advent of radio compounded Labor's fears that newspapers would control the new medium. In response to the outcry, the Bruce Nationalists Country Party government restricted the number of radio stations that could be owned by a company but consolidation continued anyway with the emergence of the Murdoch, Packer and Fairfax groups.

From the outset, Class A stations were funded from licence fees while Class B stations generated revenue from advertising. Labor wanted a government-controlled British model and no commercial broadcasting while the Nationalist Country Party government favoured the American private sector system but wanted the larger capital city (Class A) stations to subsidise smaller country town stations. When the larger stations refused, the government nationalized them as their licences expired although programming

---

[25] Jonathan Holmes, ABC online's The Drum, 8 March 2012,
[26] Victor Isaacs and Rod Kirkpatrick. *Two Hundred Years of Sydney Newspapers: A Short History*, Rural Press, 2003, P. 14.

was contracted out to private enterprise.[27]

In 1926, the Bruce government established the Hammond Royal Commission into Wireless which looked at British and American radio licensing. It rejected the creation of something akin to the British Broadcasting Corporation since, "This would really result in the creation of a Government Department whose business it would be to provide entertainment and broadcasting programmes for the people. It may be that ultimately Australia will adopt such a mode of control," it wrote, "but at the present time it does not seem wise to embark upon a system which, although only operating since the commencement of this year in Great Britain, is already receiving adverse criticism." It specifically warned that "experience already shows that when Governments are placed in charge of the means of disseminating news, they are apt to use such means for the purposes of political propaganda."[28]

Despite these concerns, in 1932, the Lyons United Australia Party turned the nationalised Class A stations into the Australian Broadcasting Commission and the ABC was born. Labor continued to be concerned however about commercial broadcasters and in the Gibson Committee (1941-42) three ALP members called for them to be nationalised.[29]

There was heavy-handed censorship of the press during both World Wars, ostensibly for security reasons, though it was often blatantly political.[30] The *Sydney Morning Herald* editorialised that Labor minister for Information, Arthur Calwell, hoped to establish

[27] Western Australia Television History watvhistory.com/2012/08/the-6wfstory-part-1-of-3.

[28] Royal Commission on Wireless, Report of the Royal Commission on Wireless, (Hammond Commission) HJ Green, Government Printer for the State of Victoria, Melbourne, 1927, p. 4.

[29] William Gerrand Gibson, Senator for Victoria, 1935-47 (Australian Country Party), The Biographical Dictionary of the Australian Senate, http://biography.senate.gov.au/index.php/gibson-william-gerrand/

[30] P Coleman 'Censorship', in B Griffen-Foley, ed., *A companion to the Australian media*, Australian Scholarly, North Melbourne, 2014, p. 87.

"an official press in Australia, under Government censorship and direction, with himself presumably playing the role of Dr. Goebbels."[31]

The Curtin Labor government's Broadcasting Act of 1942 gave government ministers the power to grant and renew licences, leading almost immediately to accusations of political patronage. It also gave the minister the power to regulate commercial broadcasters and the ABC, and it introduced programming standards and Australian content quotas.

Eventually, these powers were clawed back from government. In 1945, Richard Boyer would not accept the position of Chairman of the ABC unless Curtin issued a mandate of independence that Boyer drafted.[32] Boyer wanted the ABC to "stand solid and serene in the middle of our national life, running no campaign, seeking to persuade no opinion, but presenting the issues freely and fearlessly for the judgement of our people." In 1947, the ABC established an independent news service and in 1948 the government created an independent broadcasting regulator to remove power and patronage from the minister.

The arrival of television was a case of déjà vu all over again. The Chifley Labor government wanted to follow the BBC model, allowing only a government-funded broadcaster to operate but it lost the 1949 election and the Menzies Liberal Country Party Coalition government granted commercial TV licences to the major newspaper proprietors who, it reasoned, would have sufficient resources to cross-subsidize the new medium. Labor was predictably unhappy about further media concentration and also wanted enforceable local content quotas.

---

[31] Mr. Calwell Runs True to Form, *Sydney Morning Herald*, 12 October, 1944.
[32] Nick Cater, *The Lucky Culture and the Rise of an Australian Ruling Class,* Harper Collins, 2013, p.201.

Cross media ownership laws

When the Hawke Labor government came to power in 1983, it finally acted on Labor's fears and forced proprietors to choose between being "queens of the screen, princes of print or rajahs of radio":[33] It prevented a newspaper owner or a monopoly radio station from also owning a TV station and it abolished the rule that no owner could have more than two TV stations, replacing it with a rule that allowed an owner to reach no more than 75 percent of the audience. It also changed the rules for regional TV making those who had a monopoly compete against two other owners.

Again there were accusations of patronage. It was said Labor "wished to reward its friends in the media and punish its enemies. The changes suited Packer and Murdoch and inconvenienced Fairfax and the Herald and Weekly Times, who, it was said, had been critical of the Hawke government."[34]

The Act was amended by the Howard government in 2007 to allow greater foreign investment in TV and slightly more cross-media ownership. As a result, Fairfax bought Rural Press and acquired seven more commercial radio licences.

Labor was apoplectic with shadow communications spokesman, Stephen Conroy claiming it was "a massive handing of concentration of media ownership to the most powerful people in the land already".[35]

---

[33] Ben Goldsmith, Turnbull's media reforms might not go far enough for Murdoch's liking, The Conversation, 24 March 2015.
[34] Rob Harding-Smith, Centre for Policy Development Issue Brief, Media Ownership and Regulation in Australia, August 2011.
[35] Ibid.

Public interest test

Once Labor was returned to government, Conroy established the Convergence Review and it soon became clear that the aim was to prevent people that the government didn't consider to be 'fit and proper' from owning media outlets. As one media analyst put it, "Mrs. Rinehart's rapid move into Fairfax, as well as her earlier holdings in Ten, could force the government into tightening up the yet-to-be-defined 'public interest test'."[36]

What was the government's objection to Rinehart owning a controlling share of Fairfax? As Alan Rusbridger, editor-in-chief of *The Guardian* saw it, "Fairfax Media … (was) under siege from the multibillionaire mining magnate Gina Rinehart, who has extremely pronounced views on climate change and politics in general, and is insistent on her right to interfere with editorial policies."[37]

The fact that Rinehart would want Fairfax to succeed financially and would therefore need to retain the loyalty of existing readers as well as attracting new ones didn't seem to figure in Rusbridger's calculations, but then in the three years to 2012 the Guardian Media Group reportedly lost 100,000 pounds a day[38] so perhaps retaining and building paying customers wasn't a business principle that interested him.

As predicted, the review's major recommendation was to scrap all the previous cross-ownership rules and replace them with a requirement for a minimum number of owners and a new communications regulator who would be able to block not just mergers but any substantial shift in media ownership, of any media outlet, on any platform, if the regulator deemed the change was not

---

[36] Chris Zappone, Rinehart's Fairfax buy may delay media reforms, *Sydney Morning Herald*, 1 February, 2012.

[37] Alan Rusbridger, *The Guardian*, 25 June 2012.

[38] Time De Lisle, *The Economist*, July/August 2012.

in the public interest.

The change did not have to involve one company taking over another or to impact on market concentration. Thus it would give the government considerable scope to intimidate any proprietor it didn't like, who could be blocked from investing in the media.[39] True, the decision would be delegated to a regulator but by appointing one of its friends, the government could be reasonably sure that the regulator might share its views.

In the end, chastened by the outcry in response to both the Finkelstein and the Convergence Review, Labor's reforms amounted to little more than cutting the licence fees of free-to-air broadcasters, which was seen as seeking patronage in the lead up to the 2013 election.

Unwinding deregulation

This leaves the Turnbull Liberal National Government to deal with a hotchpotch of government regulation, almost all of which was framed by Labor's mistrust of commercial media and its fear of commercial monopolies which it has tried to counter by ensuring a diversity of ownership. Yet, Australia's small population, dispersed over a vast continent, has lent itself to concentration, and consolidation has continued despite Labor's legislative efforts.

The paradox at the heart Australia's media laws however is that regulation, by its very nature, has created barriers to entry that have reduced the number of participants in markets, creating valuable rents and powerful players, and providing ample opportunities for patronage.

As technological advance has created new means of

---

[39] Henry Ergas, Let Market Forces Determine the Future of Media, *The Australian*, 2 July 2012.

communications that have threatened, or seemed to threaten, the viability of established media, those participants have lobbied to protect their rents.

Australia could have another free-to-air (FTA) TV station but governments have yielded to the lobbying of FTAs and maintained the status quo. The transition from analogue to digital broadcasting has also freed up an enormous amount of spectrum. In the UK, this has led to the creation of over 60 digital FTA channels with increased news, children's and niche programming but not in Australia so far because that would fracture advertising markets for FTAs who have successfully persuaded governments not to upset their apple cart.[40]

So far, the one thing the Turnbull government seems certain to do, is the one thing that the Gillard government did – cut licence fees for FTA TV stations – which is being seen as an attempt by the Turnbull government, like its predecessors, to court the titans of FTA TV.

The Turnbull government has said it wants to abolish the 75 percent reach rule, which would allow mergers between metropolitan and regional broadcasters with implications for local content, particularly local news, in regional areas. The Turnbull government also proposes abolishing the two out of three rule, which prevents a company owning more than two out of three platforms in the same licence area.

Any attempt to push through these reforms, both commercially advantageous to FTAs, without addressing the anti-siphoning rules which also benefit them, would be bitterly criticized by sporting bodies and pay TV operators, principally Fox, which are both disadvantaged by them.

The anti-siphoning rules are meant to ensure that all Australians can watch certain sporting events for free, so Pay-TV owners are excluded

---

[40] Stephen King, Free-to-air television needs reform, *The Conversation*, 20 June, 2015.

from bidding for the rights to broadcast a long list of sporting events unless they are already owned by an FTA. This substantially reduces the income of the sporting bodies who have to sell the rights for less to the FTAs than if Pay-TV were also bidding. Then the FTAs on-sell many of the rights to Pay-TV. In 2010, this annual transfer from the sports bodies to the FTA owners was estimated at $100m.[41] No wonder the FTAs don't want the government to call time on such a profitable venture but under the 'just terms' provision in s 51(xxxi) of the *Australian Constitution* sports bodies should be able to recoup the financial losses they suffer under anti-siphoning laws.[42]

The internet revolution

Meanwhile, the internet has extended the reach of print, radio and television across national boundaries, driving globalisation and fracturing advertising markets. Technological change has also allowed the convergence of media platforms, with every medium accessible through ever smaller and more portable devices – from desktop computer, to laptop, iPad, iPhone, and Apple Watch.

Content is being fractured into its smallest components, particularly on social media, where participants share news, current affairs and popular culture in discrete bytes rather than watch a TV station all evening, or for a whole news broadcast, read a newspaper or listen to a radio program.

The internet and social media are also reducing the barriers of entry to zero. Suddenly, to paraphrase William Harcourt, we are all publishers now.

A study of the state of the news media in 2016 in the United

---

[41] Henry Ergas, Blowing the Final Whistle on Australian TV rules, *The Australian*, 19 November, 2010
[42] Constitutional Law Challenges to Anti-Siphoning Laws in the United States and Australia, James B. Perrine, Covington & Burlington, USA.

States shows just how devastating this trend has been for the US newspaper industry. It found that in 2015, the average weekday newspaper circulation, print and digital combined, fell by 7 percent. Weekday digital circulation increased by 2 percent but only accounted for 22 percent of the total circulation.[43] Television fared better. The combined average viewership for prime-time news on Cable TV increased 8 percent and the evening news viewership increased 1 percent.

The big winner however was digital but it didn't benefit newspapers. Their ad revenue was down 8 percent. Digital ad revenue however grew by a massive 20 percent to $60 billion and 65 percent of that was captured by five tech companies – Facebook, Google, Yahoo, Microsoft and Twitter.[44] None of these organisations produce news, which is an expensive business – they capture the profits of it without incurring costs, although they pay content providers a share of ad revenue if a piece of content generates ad revenue. But that's the problem – Google News has no ads. Google provides it as a service because it leads to users making searches on Google's main search engine that does produce ads.[45]

Yet, while the tech giants do not contribute to the production of news, increasingly they promote an editorial line. For example, former Facebook workers say news stories of interest to conservative readers were suppressed from the "trending" news section, even when they were actually trending more than other news items.[46] The sort of stories suppressed included items about Republicans such as

[43] Amy Mitchell and Jesse Holcomb, 'State of the News Media 2016', Pew Research Center Journalism & Media, 15 June 2016.
[44] Ibid.
[45] Tim Worstall, If Google News is Worth $100 Million Then Why Can't Google Pay The Newspaper Publishers?, 14 December, 2014, forbes.com.
[46] Michael Nunez, 'Former Facebook Workers: We Routinely Suppressed Conservative News', gizmodo.com, 5 September 2016

Mitt Romney or Ted Cruz, inappropriate scrutiny of conservatives by the tax office, or stories that came from conservative outlets such as Fox News, Breitbart or Newsmax.[47] At the same time, stories would be "injected" into the so-called trending news section that weren't trending such as news about the Black Lives Matter campaign.[48]

The same broad trends are occurring in Australia. Printed newspaper circulation declined rapidly with industry revenue declining at an annualized 8.4 percent over the last five years and 5.7 percent in 2015-16 as readers switched to online content.[49]

Television is holding up better. Although most households own numerous screens, the majority internet-capable and many portable, on average 88 per cent of Australians watch some broadcast TV (FTA or Pay-Tv) on in-home sets each week; the average amount watched is 90 hours per month, live TV is the dominant activity, and 86 percent of viewing is TV content watched within 28 days of broadcast.[50]

As for social media, more than 1.04 billion people use Facebook worldwide and in Australia, Facebook has a staggering 15 million users. This dwarfs the level of penetration of its competitors – Twitter has only 2.8 million users in Australia.[51]

Diversity in Public broadcasting

The great irony of Australian media regulation is that as the government contemplates how it will regulate commercial media to avoid media concentration and ensure a diversity of voices, it overlooks the lack

[47] Ibid.
[48] Ibid.
[49] Newspaper Publishing Market Research Report, ANZSIC J5411 June 2016, ibisworld.com.au.
[50] Q2 2016 Australian Multi-Screen Report Shows Collective Influence of New Opportunities To View, Oztam, Regional TAM, Nielsen, 6 October 2016.
[51] David Cowling, 'Social Media Statistics Australia September 2016', 1 October, 2016, SocialMediaNews.com.au

of diversity in public broadcasting. The Fraser Liberal Country Party government, no fan of the ABC, introduced the only diversity of ownership with the creation of the Special Broadcasting Service in 1978.

The elephant in the room is the ABC, which is required to have national reach and operate across every platform, even competing with print media in the online space, as well as offering online video, audio, podcasts, TV programs on-demand, and reaching out to audiences through Facebook, Twitter, YouTube, Flickr and Instagram.

This multi-platform leviathan is committed to every sort of diversity imaginable except the one that really matters – the diversity of ideas. Thus when Michelle Guthrie, the newly appointed managing director of the ABC, was asked whether the ABC was "overly 'reflective' of left-wing opinion" she responded, "I don't see that as true at all. People view any organisation from their own biases and my sense is that we do a very good job in covering the gamut of opinion."[52]

Really? There is an enormous amount of evidence to the contrary. The Institute of Public Affairs, for example, has published three papers that question the ability of the ABC to deliver objective news content. In one, the IPA commissioned independent media monitoring company iSentia to analyse ABC coverage of energy policy issues. iSentia examined more than 2,350 separate ABC reports from September 2013 to March 2014 and found consistent systemic bias across all platforms and regions. For example, 52 percent of renewable energy stories were favourable and only 10 per cent unfavourable. The rest were neutral. By comparison, just 15 percent of stories about coal mining were favourable and 31 percent were unfavourable and only 12 percent of coal seam gas stories were favourable and 43 percent

---

[52] Megan Lehmann, ABC managing director Michelle Guthrie addresses bias claims, *The Australian*, 27 May, 2016.

were unfavourable.[53]

A decade ago, when Mark Scott became managing director of the ABC he announced that he had listened to the critics of the ABC's "editorial perspective … (and its) issues with balance – and fairness – particularly through its news and current affairs content although some critics would suggest, across its entire content,"[54] and he committed to, deliver "balance, diversity, impartiality" and to ensure that ABC audiences could "see and hear a broad range of viewpoints on matters of importance".[55]

A decade later, Jonathan Holmes delivered his verdict writing, that it was "undeniable … that the ABC's capital city radio presenters come across, overwhelmingly, as leaning more to the left than the right," and adding, "I say "undeniably", but senior ABC managers for decades have chosen, if not to deny it, then to ignore it, and they've certainly failed to do anything about it."[56]

Holmes says there is a "good commercial rationale" for this bias because it fills "a gap in the market" arguing "it's even harder to find a left-wing presenter on commercial talk radio than it is to find a right-winger on the ABC".[57]

In reality, it's almost impossible for commercial competitors to compete with the ABC's taxpayer funded, left-leaning offerings. That's certainly what Crikey publisher Eric Beecher wrote attacking the ABC for branching into online commentary in competition his website, which he likened to seeing "tanks roll up on our lawn".[58] ABC news

---

[53] James Paterson, Independent report reveals ABC biased against fossil fuels, 11 August 2014.

[54] Mark Scott, The Editorial Values of the ABC, *The Sydney Papers*, Summer 2007, P. 66.

[55] Ibid, P.68 – 69.

[56] Jonathan Holmes, ABC radio personalities need to tune out their left-wing bias, *Sydney Morning Herald*, 5 April 2016.

[57] Ibid.

[58] Lara Sinclair, Crikey! Publisher Eric Beecher lashes the ABC, *The Australian*, 11 October, 2010.

and commentary online make it harder for all newspaper to generate revenue, particularly Fairfax papers and *Guardian Australia* and ABC News 24 draws away viewers from Sky News.

As Holmes writes:

> If the ABC wasn't funded by taxpayer dollars, no one would mind … But the ABC is publicly funded. It does have a legal obligation to not favour one point of view over another… The leftiness of ABC radio output is doubly problematic when it comes to Radio National … (because) it doesn't have commercial competition… if I were a supporter of Tony Abbott, or even of John Howard, I would feel that the vast bulk of RN's output was not for me … For decades, Coalition senators have been asking ABC managing directors at estimates hearings: "Where is the right-wing Phillip Adams?" The ABC's answer has been to give half an hour here and there on Radio National to the likes of Amanda Vanstone and Tom Switzer – neither of them more than mildly right of centre. Frankly, it is little better than mockery.[59]

Yet as Scott says, under Section 8 of the ABC Act, the corporation is obliged to be "independent, accurate and impartial."[60]

> Unlike some of the commercial media, we have to serve *all* of the public, not just those who would come to the ABC for comfort or confirmation. We're not here to hold anyone's hand, but to confront, challenge and explore a broad range of views.[61]

Unfortunately, the ABC's most recent annual report shows that there has been a steady increase in dissatisfaction with the ABC and almost one quarter of all Australians (23 percent) think the ABC is not balanced and even-handed when reporting news and current affairs

---

[59] Jonathan Holmes, ABC radio personalities need to tune out their left-wing bias, *Sydney Morning Herald*, 5 April 2016.
[60] Mark Scott, The Editorial Values of the ABC, *The Sydney Papers*, Summer 2007, P. 73.
[61] Ibid.

and almost one third (31 percent) think the ABC is not efficient and well managed.[62]

Complaints about election coverage in 2015 showed that more than twice as many people complained that election coverage in NSW and Victoria was biased in favour of Labor compared with coverage of the Coalition, and almost twice as many in Queensland thought the bias was in favour of Labor rather than the Coalition.[63]

In addition, there were more than 5,500 complaints about bias, inaccuracy and lack of balance and almost 25,000 about program standards.[64]

One hopes that Guthrie might take note but Holmes warns that if she wants to tackle the issue, she'll have her work cut out for her. "She'll be facing an entrenched culture within the ABC. Many of its staff genuinely think that most well-informed people think as they do".[65]

Guthrie however thinks the problem lies elsewhere. "I feel we do have a lot of editorial processes in place and we just need to make sure we adhere to them. I feel very confident those processes are well adhered to."

In an email to employees, she wrote, "We must extend our reach and our relevance into areas where we are under-represented. That means more diversity in both our staff and our content."[66] What sort of diversity? Ethnic. News, radio, television and online departments must increase content makers from ethnic backgrounds from 7.4 per cent to 12 per cent by 2018.[67]

---

[62] All About Audiences, ABC Annual Report, 6 October, 2015, P. 29.

[63] Ibid, P. 74.

[64] Ibid, P. 117.

[65] Jonathan Holmes, ABC radio personalities need to tune out their left-wing bias, *Sydney Morning Herald*, 5 April 2016.

[66] Jake Mitchell, *The Australian*, May 2, 2016.

[67] Paul Cleary, ABC order big rise in ethnic-background journos, *The Australian*, 17 October, 2016.

That will please one critic who mocked ABC programmes for showing "white people selling antiques, an ivory woman hosting the news, an eggshell woman hosting another news program, a cream British comedian hosting a panel show, a vanilla Australian comedian hosting a satirical news program and a comedy pilot starring a ghost woman produced by the Asian guys from the Chaser, the Caucasian guys."[68] For such people all the ABC needs to do is replace Leigh Sales with Lee Lin Chin and Michelle Guthrie's your Aunty.

Outgoing managing director Mark Scott, in his final days at the national broadcaster called for targets for gender diversity and said "we are pushing for more diversity in our staff (but) frankly, I don't think we do as well in that area as the BBC."[69] Indeed. The BBC is embracing the alphabet soup of identity politics pledging that by 2020 half of its workforce and leadership will be female and 15 percent BAME, that is black, Asian and minority ethnic, 8 percent will be disabled and 8 per cent will be LGBT – lesbian, gay, bisexual or transgender.[70] One wonders how one will have to prove one's sexual orientation – will self-identification be sufficient? How black, Asian or minority ethnic will one have to be? Can one be a fair-skinned black with blonde hair and blue eyes?

The face of change at the BBC is not that of seasoned professionals like its Director-General, Lord Tony Hall of Birkenhead who rose through the ranks working on key news programs including the *World at One*, the Nine O'clock News and *Newsnight*, but Tunde Ogungbesan, the recently appointed head of Diversity, Inclusion and Succession who is leading the BBC's diversity and inclusion strategy for staff and on-screen portrayal and developing "diversity commissioning guidelines ... to ensure that anyone who makes programmes for (the

---

[68] Dan Ilic, Diversity at the ABC – The Feed, SBS2, 3 May, 2016.
[69] Michael Bodey, *The Australian,* 27 April, 2016.
[70] BBC launches ambitious new diversity and inclusion strategy, BBC Media Centre, 28 April, 2016

BBC) shares our values and commitments."[71]

But how does one combine a commitment to diversity with a policy that ensures that everyone shares the same values and commitments? Clearly, there is no room for diversity in values and commitments so who determines what the shared values and commitments should be? In Australia, the Board of the ABC is responsible but from the outset it has been making excuses. For example, the first Chairman, Charles Lloyd Jones, said that because of its colonial culture, the ABC could not compete with "the high broadcast standards of London."[72]

Importantly, whereas the BBC's Royal Charter and Agreement go into great detail about what the BBC does, how it is funded and how it should serve audiences, the Charter of the ABC is a few hundred words long and while the BBC Charter is reviewed in detail every 10 years, the ABC Charter has received haphazard attention.

The Charter simply says that the ABC should provide "innovative and comprehensive broadcasting services of a high standard" including programs that "contribute to a sense of national identity and inform and entertain, and reflect the cultural diversity of, the Australian community" and "programs of an educational nature." It must also "provide digital media services" and "encourage and promote the musical, dramatic and performing arts in Australia."

In broadcasting, "the Corporation shall take account of: (i) the broadcasting services provided by the commercial and community sectors ... (iii) the responsibility of the Corporation as the provider of an independent national broadcasting service to provide a balance between broadcasting programs of wide appeal and specialized broadcasting programs; (and) (iv) the multicultural character of the Australian community ..."

---

[71] Ibid.
[72] Ibid.

Within this sketchiest of frameworks, the ABC can do as it pleases with virtual impunity. The Charter specifically stipulates that, nothing in it "shall be taken 'to impose on the Corporation a duty that is enforceable by proceedings in a court". Neither is it subject to consumer pressure; one cannot, as one can in Britain, cancel one's subscription since the Chifley Labor government decided to fund the ABC directly from general revenue and the Whitlam Labor government abolished the fees altogether in 1973.

In Britain, the GBP 145.50 licence fee continues to provide the bulk of funding for the BBC,[73] forcing it to be more conscious of the viewing public. The next largest source of funding is commercial income, largely sales of BBC programs internationally, which drives the BBC to provide programs of a very high standard. The BBC gets a subsidy from the government but this will be fully phased out by 2021 when it is expected to be worth around GBP750 million out of anticipated revenue of GBP 4.8 billion.

American public broadcasting, by contrast, is largely decentralised and relies on individual subscriptions, on-air and online pledge drives, the sale of spots to sponsors – although there are strict conditions limiting acknowledgements so that they cannot advertise – and a small amount of government funding. Public television and radio stations like PBS and NPR got a mere $445 million in 2012, about 0.014 of the US federal budget, and this was provided to the Corporation on Public Broadcasting, which provides a small amount to around 580 local TV and radio stations and the rest to programming, which the stations pay to run.[74] The main justification for public funding is that the programming is educational and sometimes the only educational programming in poor regional and rural areas.

---

[73] Stu Wood, BBC Struggles with Series of Woes, *Wall Street Journal*, 13 October 2016.
[74] Brad Plumer, Why exactly should the government fund PBS and NPR?, *Washington Post*, 10 October 2012.

In comparing the media in Australia with Britain and the US it is striking how, despite the differences in structure and funding, there is a similarity in the values of the media elite in each country. There is a recognizable common culture between the ABC and the BBC which is unsurprising giving the extent to which the ABC has been modelled on the BBC.

As for the US, in 2010, Angelo Codevilla described the emergence of an American ruling class over the previous decades, which is comprised largely of people working in government and their allies in the media.[75] 'Its first tenet,' he wrote, 'is that "we" are the best and brightest while the rest of Americans are retrograde, racist, and dysfunctional unless properly constrained.'

In *The Lucky Culture – The Rise of an Australian Ruling Class*, Nick Cater outlined the rise of a similar class in Australia whose worldview dominates in the nation's key cultural citadels – the universities, the arts establishments and the ABC.[76]

Unfortunately, this ruling class can be petty and intolerant. As Orwell wrote, "it is the liberals who fear liberty and the intellectuals who want to do dirt on the intellect…"[77] And they are empowered not just by illiberal laws but by seemingly unquenchable rivers of taxpayer funding that flow to their ivory towers.

The fracturing of commercial media revenue models has meant that those who have been able to retain privileged access to mass markets, thanks to government legislation, have captured valuable rents – transparently, in the case of the ABC, or opaquely, in the case of free-to-air TV – and as a result they wield enormous political power, which they unashamedly use to try to entrench their privileges

---

[75] Angelo M. Codevilla, *The American Spectator,* 16 July 2010

[76] Nick Cater, *The Lucky Culture – The Rise of an Australian Ruling Class,* Harper Collins, 2013.

[77] George Orwell: 'The Freedom of the Press' First published: *The Times Literary Supplement,* September 15, 1972.

and the status quo. Fear of the power these publicly-subsidised media magnates wield explains, more than anything else, why the party of liberalism has been as feeble in rolling back statist encroachments on individual liberty as Labor, which believes in statism.

Where to from here?

It is high time we overcame the long-held anxiety about the threat of commercial media monopolies. The era of digital media abundance is providing many more viewing options that compete with mainstream commercial players. The real challenge to diversity is the cultural monopoly of a monolithic public broadcaster with a loose remit and limited accountability. It transmits in colour but speaks in monotone.

Calls for the ABC to be privatised or scrapped are appealing to many on the centre right but by no means all – there has always been strong support for public broadcasting among some on the right, particularly in regional and rural Australia, just as there is concern about ensuring sufficient reporting of news and current affairs outside the major metropolises. Yet even among those on the Right who support public broadcasting there is concern about balance and bias.

The best way to bring fresh air and ideas into public broadcasting and break down the groupthink is to break down the monolithic structure of the ABC and increase contestability in the production of programming.

The review of the BBC Charter has recommended the establishment of "a new contestable public service content fund to create new opportunities for others to provide the best public service broadcasting content in the UK and enhance plurality in the provision of public service content."[78] We should do the same here.

---

[78] A BBC For The Future: A Broadcaster Of Distinction, John Whittingdale, Secretary of State for Culture, Media and Sport, May 2016, P. 6

There are also plans for the BBC to spin-off its in-house production into a new subsidiary, BBC Studios, to produce programmes for the BBC and other broadcasters in the UK and internationally.[79] The ABC should do likewise.

Instead of tying taxpayer money to a gargantuan bureaucracy, funding should be allocated for particular television services – such as children's educational programs, news and current affairs, Australian history, or Australian drama.

Competitors should bid on a level playing field to run a specific channel – News 24 for example – just as the Gillard government put the running of Australia TV out to tender and received bids from the ABC and Sky TV. Requirements should include ensuring balance in the coverage of news and current affairs.

Allocating funding specifically for a regional, rural and remote service, or services, which were put out to tender, would remove the need for specific local content requirements in regional areas.

Production companies could also team up with a TV station to bid for funding for a particular program or series of programs, for example, Australian history or drama, which could be run on any free-to-air station in prime time.

With Australian content funded in this way, there would be no need for general Australian content requirements but programs funded in this way should not have advertising breaks even if they ran on commercial TV.

Independent production companies already bid for funding and some of the ABC's best programs are already made this way, such as 'Changing Minds' and 'Choir of Hard Knocks', just as some of America's most successful programs – such as Sesame Street – have been produced by PBS without a costly behemoth like the ABC.

---

[79] Ibid.

There are a number of things the government should do which would be of great benefit for the FTA TV stations. Apart from removing local and regional content rules, all media cross-ownership laws should be rescinded – if they ever made sense, they certainly don't in an age when people can access print, radio, TV, films, video and music from around the world. FTA licence fees should also be reduced or abolished but all this should be done as part of a trade-off for changes to broadcast licences.

First, around half the spectrum that each FTA has should be withdrawn – technological advances have dramatically reduced the spectrum required for broadcasting and FTAs use around half the spectrum they are allocated for low quality programs.[80]

The new licence would give them ownership of the spectrum they retain, which they could use to broadcast FTA TV, rent to others who wish to broadcast, or sell. The spectrum that was returned to the government and the spectrum that has been set aside for a sixth FTA should be auctioned off for TV, telephony or other uses.[81]

Specialist broadcasters could apply, at minimum cost, for a new content service license and bid for capacity on spectrum held by the FTAs or the government, without having to own and operate an FTA TV station themselves.[82]

The government should recognize that its anti-siphoning list imposes a heavy cost on sports organisations and pay fair compensation for reducing their income. This should prompt it to evaluate the costs and benefits of insisting that such a wide range of events be on the anti-siphoning list, including some that are never broadcast on FTA.

Finally, it is intolerable that the RDA is being used to punish journalists and cartoonists in Kafkaesque trials. It illustrates how

---

[80] Stephen King, Free-to-air television needs reform, The Conversation, 20 June, 2015.
[81] Ibid.
[82] Ibid.

dangerous it is to legislate about something as ill-defined, subjective and trivial as offence, insults and humiliation. Given that threatening or inciting racially or religiously motivated violence is already illegal under criminal law, Sections 18c and 18d of the RDA should be repealed as soon as possible.

Last, despite the encroachments of government and the threats of Islamists, this is a golden age for media freedom. Never in the history of humanity have so many people had so much time to read and had access to so much written material. Never before have so many been able to write. Never has it been easier to research or to publish. So there has never been a better time, or in Australia, a safer place, for classical liberals to make the case for the removal of government-funded monopolies and to stand up for free speech and a free press.

Orwell wrote, "If liberty means anything at all it means the right to tell people what they do not want to hear. The common people still vaguely subscribe to that doctrine and act on it."[83] The most visible threat to media freedom in Australia today is a kangaroo commissioner menacing a cartoonist. When the political class finally realise that the cartoonist has the common people on his side they may summon up the courage to change the law. If they are looking for a precedent, there is no finer one than Francis Forbes – it's time to vanquish the ghost of Governor Darling once again.

---

[83] Ibid.

Industrial Relations Reform Must Follow the Money

Graeme Haycroft

Graeme Haycroft used to employ over 2000 people across 150 or so businesses before he retired from his labour hire/IR consultancy

It is not possible to write sensibly about industrial relations (IR) in Australia without understanding its significance for the tribal left. The IR game is not only the primary source of funds for the those of the tribe who live directly or indirectly off government, its myths link them with working folk who pay the taxes, and other extractions, that support the career left.

It always pays to follow the money.

The unions, by virtue of their legally privileged monopoly, collect money from members. This money is then used to support the Labor party, who do whatever is necessary to maintain the union monopoly, and the effective compulsory membership of members, so the funds can keep flowing.

The myths are such good cover, Coalition politicians have never shown any understanding of the underlying pattern.

Yet everyone on the left understands how important this business model is for the tribe's survival. Every institution that potentially could bring pressure to bear to protect this cash flow has been enlisted in this cause. They all happily promote and protect the myth that unions exist to protect their workers and what they do to that end, irrespective of how they might do it, is all being done for a good cause: their cause.

The traditional IR system, with its iconic symbolism of penalty rates, redundancy, overtime rates, sick and personal leaves, long service leave and, more recently, maternity leave, serve to unite the two broad constituencies of the Labor party. The first group is the socially conservative blue-collar workers, whose incomes are significantly reduced by the added cost of the imposition of ideological icons required under the left-sustaining IR regime. After all, they mostly work in competitive environments, where unit labour costs matter. Given the choice (which most would like to have but is denied to them), most would happily trade all the IR icons for money in the hand. It's all about the bottom line for them.

The other group in this Labor constituency are largely employed by the government or in sectors that depend upon the government. The cost of their IR icons are met by the taxpayer, either directly or as costs passed on by their protected employers.

Authoritarian, "we know what's best for you" -ism, is part of their collectivist credo. Most of them believe that the first group would not be capable of exercising choice in their own best interests, so they are opposed on those grounds alone to allowing the first group the choice they would prefer.

As for themselves, they are all very busy saving the planet, promoting gay marriage, teaching young children safe schools curriculum, supporting unrestricted immigration and all the other fashionable left wing causes. All their friends and acquaintances passionately believe in, and espouse the importance of, the IR icons. They would risk social ostracism to question the status quo. If it's (mythically) good for the workers, it is also good for them.

We are speaking of general trends, of course, but unless you have a general understanding of the current context of IR in Australia, and what forces would be unleashed if any change is proposed to the system, then reform will fail, as it always has in the past.

IR reform has very little to do with changes in the workplace and almost everything to do with the continued control by the left of institutions, including within government. So, the first order of business for reform is to dry up the supply of money that feeds this control.

Understanding the model

The union movement funds the political and quasi-political system with tens of millions of dollars each year.

They have two huge advantages, mostly by virtue of culture rather than specific legislation. The first is that an employee, for instance, is not allowed to negotiate his or her own workplace agreement. This used to be the exclusive monopoly preserve of the registered unions until, uncharacteristically, the *Fair Work Act* allowed each worker to appoint his or her own agent, which may be a union or another party or person. Employees still can't do it themselves but at least this means that the way is now clear for alternate employee representation bodies, albeit unregistered ones, to compete in this space.

First to do this was Queensland ambulance officer Sid Cramp, now an LNP State parliamentarian. In 2005, he and a few of his ambulance officer friends started an alternative association for Queensland paramedics called EMSPA (now called APAQ in Queensland).

Although there are probably only ten or twelve thousand paramedics in Australia, the apolitical lower cost better service EMSPA/APAQ now has three or four times the membership in the eastern states amongst paramedics than the traditional monopoly union, United Voice.

In 2014, inspired by Sid's work, another group started an alternative nurses' union in Queensland (NPAQ) providing the same service as the QNU but with membership at almost half the price and an avowedly apolitical approach. It too is growing rapidly. Here is how the numbers work. There are 345,000 nurse members Australia-wide in the existing nurses' unions. Their new competitors only have to get about 10-15% of those members in just one state before the traditional unions have to slash their fees Australia-wide to match them. This will wipe $50 million from their cash flow. Similar numbers would apply to teachers and the teachers' unions. These new start-ups will dramatically restrict the flow of money to the Labor/left causes, but a hundred times more importantly, it will allow the moderate and commonsense voices of nurses and teachers back into the health and education policy debate in this country. Protection without politics is a winning theme.

The second advantage is that only registered unions can do special deals with employers that reduce the "award" entitlements. As the Royal Commission into Construction Unions shows, if any person or organisation has a special power that no-one else possesses to save or make money for another party, then the party with that power can demand a reward from the party that benefits.

It is instructive to look at how this legal privilege is used by the

Shoppies union (the SDA) and Coles and Woolworths to their mutual advantage. The *Fair Work Act* grants the SDA certain powers that are not available to others. However, and far more importantly, the institution that regulates how those powers are interpreted, the Fair Work Commission (FWC), has been stacked over time with people who understand that their livelihoods, and those of their tribe, are preserved by interpretations which maintain the status quo.

The SDA has turned these special powers into tens of millions of dollars worth of support for the tribal left and the Labor party each year. The SDA has agreed to workplace arrangements for Coles and Woolworths that dramatically reduce the impact of penalty rates, and substantially reduces unit labour costs for Coles and Woolworths. These retail giants control 70-80% of retail trade in Australia. Having workplace arrangements like this is a huge advantage to them – provided it is not also available to their smaller competitors. So, in return for the SDA not negotiating the similar deal with Coles' and Woolworths' competitors, Coles and Woolworths happily ensure that every one of their 250,000 or so employees joins the SDA.

Do the maths. With an average membership fee of say $300 per year ... 250,000 x $300 = $75 million. But blind Freddy could easily run a union like SDA for $15-20 million and still provide a better service for members.

There is a sea of money flowing to the SDA. It doesn't need any contracts or memorandums of understanding with Coles, or Woolworths – money speaks its own language. When IGA tried to register an agreement with similar conditions as Coles and Woolworths, the SDA went into the FWC and opposed it. They had about 75 million reasons each year to do so.

A challenge to the Coles workplace agreement has been successfully made by a disgruntled and determined employee of

Coles Duncan Hart, who pointed out to the FWC what everybody already knew and had turned a blind eye to. This was that the Coles workplace agreement should not have been approved in the first place. Nor indeed should any of its predecessor agreements. As a result of the publicity, the FWC had to agree.

The issue is, at the time of writing, still in a state of flux with further challenges pending. Logic suggests that ultimately all of the Coles' and Woolworths' workplace agreements will be rejected and all their employees forced back to the iconic award. That might thrill the ideological left but horrify everyone else, but most importantly Coles and Woolworths would no longer have a commercial advantage that gives them an incentive to keep insisting their employees join the SDA. The SDA would lose 90% of its income and nothing would flow to the Labor party or other pet left-wing projects.

Let me predict that this won't happen because money has always talked louder than logic in industrial relations. Every force in the left will be brought to bear to keep the money flowing. It will all just quietly go away.

You see Labor and the left understand how important the Labor/union model is to their continued survival.

What is to be done?

So how do you stop all this? There is certainly no set of laws that could ever be introduced that would get past a Senate controlled by the beneficiaries of this system and believers in its myths.

So you either remove the powers completely, so that no-one has them, or you allow virtually anyone to have those special powers so the political rents can be competed away.

The underlying problem is that, to some extent, the power for alternative agencies or organisations to do what a union does now already exists, yet the real exercise of this "special union negotiating power" is the gift of the appointees of the FWC, all of whom understand that their careers depend on the retention of these powers.

In practical terms, as we discovered in the Heydon Royal Commission, when AWU (Australian Workers Union) Secretary Bill Shorten presented his EBAs (Enterprise Bargaining Agreements) to the FWC for "Clean Event" and "Chiquita Mushrooms", the respective Fair Work Commissioners applied standard practice and simply did not check anything closely. If any other party had lodged an identical EBA for the same employers they would have been knocked back.

We also know that Bill Shorten had accepted contributions to his personal political campaign fund from those grateful employers who had been granted a competitive advantage by him. Somehow he had forgotten to declare that to his members.

But the culture was, and still is, that no FW Commissioner ever critically looks at the agreements lodged by the registered unions. Changing this culture is not going to be easy, yet understanding it is the first step.

So it is pretty clear that reform of the system will not come from its beneficiaries in the Senate. If there is a way forward it will be at the State and not the Federal level, one that prioritizes the Coalition's core small business constituency. All this is perfectly and easily doable.

There is also another huge election-winning and government-maintaining constituency, once the bulwark of the Labor party but now being abandoned by them – the socially conservative blue collar workers. The employee tradies, blue-collar professionals such as paramedics (as Sid Cramp showed), nurses and even a significant proportion of teachers. The employees of small businesses are also ripe for the picking if Pauline Hanson doesn't do it first.

They are all waiting for a political party who will trust them and support their rights to make the choices that they want to make. The employees of small businesses are not generally unionised, but all the blue collar and salaried professionals, including teachers, are in unions, not because they like the ideology but because it is an effective condition of employment to have the professional indemnity cover that they get from the unions. They currently do not have a choice as to who will represent them but would welcome it if a choice were given to them, especially if it were cheaper, better and apolitical.

Past and current Coalition IR policy has always patronised workers. It was skewed towards the IR club view of the world that Labor looked after the unions, which were bad, and the Coalition looked after the industry associations, which were good.

Yet, industry associations contribute virtually nothing financially to the Coalition, but openly support, and are beneficiaries of, the union/Labor business cash-flow model. They avowedly want no change.

A winning political party has to craft coherent constituencies that will give it the numbers. There is a strong community of interest with a common uniting theme "give the workers choice, and let the workers decide". The coalition has to understand that choice is good and patronizing is bad. Associations of employees or unions are good but that it is the *monopoly* that the existing unions hold that is bad. Hence alternative unions have to be allowed to set up under the credo that the sole determinant of which union or association a worker may join will be made by the worker and no-one other than the worker.

All this, however, is extremely difficult to achieve. Labor politicians know that restrictive rules help their cause, so they happily make them. Coalition politicians rarely understand this. They universally want to make rules to demonstrate how caring they are about protecting workers. Being patronising is seen as a worthy characteristic in the Coalition parliamentary circles because it tends to give immediate gratification. Furthermore, it silences the criticisms of the left whose supporters are of course terrified of the consequences of allowing workers actual choice.

Managing this is not going to be easy. Any new unions or employee associations must not be registered as unions. A Coalition government must move the opposite way and insist that the existing registered unions simply comply with federal ASIC or each State's respective association and incorporation rules.

There is an argument that the disclosure rules for representative organisations be tightened up to make them transparent to their members but this distracts from the core issue of allowing the workers the sole right of choice. If you are offering choice to workers, you have to trust workers are capable of exercising that choice. The value of an organisation's service to a member in a competitive environment will have little or nothing to do with the members' knowledge of the financial workings of the organisation. Commercial reality will force organisations to be transparent. As long as there is competition, and the members have free choice, you don't need special rules. There are only four broad principles that a Coalition State government would have to follow for these policies to be effective.

1. The government should only deal or negotiate with employee organisations that are registered under the existing State associations incorporation rules or its federal counterpart for association in ASIC. There must

be no special registrations or rules, the same rules that apply to thousands of other voluntary associations should apply to all employee associations.

2. Remove all provisions in the respective State industrial relations Acts that grant monopoly representation rights to any employee or employer organisation.

3. Make a policy announcement that all government employee negotiations will be decentralized and done where possible on an enterprise or regional basis.

4. As the employee status quo should be the default position in any negotiation, any agreement that employees have voted on does not need to be ratified by any other body. The status quo is the protection.

Note that, if all existing agreements were automatically CPI (Consumer Price Index) indexed, no worker could ever be disadvantaged by artificial protraction of negotiations. In fact, most agreements would probably not need re-negotiating, thereby eliminating one of the traditional roles of the unions.

The only role left for the Industrial Relations Commission, which would no longer need to adjudicate on the creation of agreements, would be to arbitrate, adjudicate, conciliate (or whatever other PC terms are in vogue) for actual disputes between employees and their employers in terms of their respective agreements.

There are the usual hoary arguments that will be trawled out such as "with more than one union who is the government going to deal with?". Oh my gosh, what a dilemma. Every other employer in the land knows that it has to deal with its own employees because it is they who do the work. Any representative organisation, new or old, is simply there to help its members. All of them have to be dealt with. The blue collar constituency that is looking for a new political home will respond to the call that it is the workers that the government will deal with and it is the workers, not their representative associations, who will decide.

There are two other important policy areas that the State government can effectively implement to break the union/Labor business cash flow model.

1: Small Business IR reform.

The Coalition state governments can all recover (even Victoria) the constitutional IR powers. Now, whilst this ostensibly applies to non-corporations and most small businesses are incorporated, these state industrial relations powers can, in practice, be made to apply to all small businesses who collectively employ approximately half of each state's total employees. I define small business as family-owned and controlled businesses and not public companies. One of the core constituencies of the coalition is the owners and families of these businesses. But the families whose livelihoods depend upon these businesses will also vote Coalition, if they are treated with respect by a Coalition government.

Because the workplace culture in small businesses is so markedly different from big businesses, using the existing status quo as the default position for employee conditions, a Coalition state government could legislate to allow employers and employees to negotiate "individual flexibility agreements" ("IFAs") along the lines set out by Julia Gillard in the FW Act when she was Labor's IR minister. They will not be copying the hated "workchoices" but the much loved "Gillard Labor" policies.

Small business employers and employees could negotiate change to workplace conditions in writing which don't have to be registered. Workers will happily trade things like penalty rates for things they value more, such as better continuity of roster hours, provided that it is their decision and theirs alone to do so.

For instance, if a worker enters into such an arrangement and one week later feels for any reason that he or she has been "exploited", then he or she can end it after the next pay period and go back to the conditions he or she was on before. There is no need for any third party assessment of such arrangements.

Up to 50% of each State's workforce will quickly climb on board such a simple and open system. It will not however apply to the management and staff of public companies who will remain under the dysfunctional Federal jurisdiction. By and large, they are part of the Labor party constituency so there is no point in the Coalition spending time worrying about a group who are not their constituency and never will be.

2: Building Industry reform.

State governments do about 80-90% of all government construction and development. The industry is dominated by the so-called "Tier 1" building cartel, headed by Lend Lease and Leighton Holdings. Nearly every other major builder in the country is tied by contract or shareholding to one of these two. There are really very few other major competitors to this group and it is the role of the CFMEU (Construction, Forestry, Mining and Energy Union) principally, and the building industry associations led by the MBA (Master Builders Association), to ensure it stays that way. It is a very unhappy marriage, but all the parties understand that their mutual self-interest is best served by staying together.

In general, this is how the game works. The CFMEU and the other building trade unions, such as the ETU (Electrical Trades Union), negotiate otherwise commercially unrealistic EBA worksite conditions. The building worker employees do very nicely thank you very much. The employers know they can pass on all these costs because the governments will only deal with the Tier 1 construction companies on major projects. The role of the MBA and the other building industry associations which are all controlled by the major building contractors, is to ensure that all the other builders and potential sub-contractors sign up to the same uncompetitive conditions with the unions. Any subcontractor who doesn't toe the line will never be allowed onto a "Tier 1" building site.

The net effect of this cartel arrangement is that about 30% is added onto the construction cost of every government project, so for every $4.3 billion of government building and construction about $1 billion is going to:

- the shareholders of the Tier 1 construction companies

- the workers on the sites

- the CFMEU and the other unions

- the MBA and the other building industry associations

The CFMEU in particular is a major contributor to the Labor and Green parties to ensure that the system isn't changed. Again, the solution is simple and no it is not to have another bunch of bureaucrats in a state building and construction commission. The Coalition needs to take a lead from the Labor party. In the ACT, the Labor government has mandated that in order to tender for any ACT government work that the tenderer must have "union-friendly" workplace arrangements (read uncompetitive provisions) which, of course, increase the tender prices but guarantee a feed of money to the unions which finds its way back to the Labor party.

The Coalition State governments have to follow this example, but with one important difference. Instead of only allowing tenderers who have uncompetitive workplace arrangements, the Coalition State governments must simply strike those tenderers who have uncompetitive provisions off the tender list. This will require Coalition Ministers with "cajones", an oxymoron if ever there was one. We can only hope.

Currently, every large builder and subcontractor in the land has these uncompetitive provisions, so until new firms are started without those friendly CFMEU arrangements, all of which add about 30% to the construction costs, all new construction projects will just have to go on pause. Commercial reality will force Lend Lease and Leighton Holdings to come to the party and end their arrangements with the CFMEU.

Passing laws to control delinquent organisations like the CFMEU, apart from not targeting the root cause of the problem, is just a waste of time.

Conclusion

So that's the plan. Keep it at the State level, trust the workers, keep it simple, and concentrate on the main game; destroying the union/ Labor business cash-flow model and working on attracting a new constituency to the Coalition whilst looking after the one that they are so grievously abandoning.

The State of our Universities

James Allan

Garrick Professor of Law at the University of Queensland

I have written elsewhere about the poor state of Australia's universities. Let me begin this chapter, nevertheless, by simply touching on a few highlights, or rather lowlights. First off, we have the Anglosphere's most centralised and bureaucratic universities. Over 60 percent of employees at all Australian universities are doing something other than lecturing and publishing. They are non-academics, some sort of administrators. To adapt the language of psychiatry, 'this is crazy'. And it's not just low level administrators there to fawn over every academic's needs. In fact those sort of administrators seem to be an endangered species. Before I came to Australia, and based on the solid groundings of the concept of comparative advantage, I never entered marks, or put exams into alphabetical order, or did those sorts of clerical tasks. It is now commonplace to have the professors do it. The explosion of administrators is at the top and middle of universities. There are marketers; supposed teaching gurus; grant-getting advisors; those devoted to furthering 'diversity'; etcetera, etcetera. And it is so top-down in Australian universities that in my eleven years I do not recall a single time when our law school got to make a single important decision on anything by having a meeting and voting. Now that's how it was when I worked in New Zealand. And in Hong Kong. And in both Canada and the US in 2013. There we used to make decisions that mattered. But not here. In Australian universities the centralisation, the top-down management structure, the one-size-fits-all approach rivals General Motors in the 1950s, or maybe the former East Germany.

I have been writing since the Coalition came into office in 2013 with suggestions about how to start to tackle these problems (in the clearly delusional hope that there is any interest in doing so on the right side of politics). Here's a good place to begin. Make every single Australian university publish the number of employees who actually teach and research as a percentage of total employment. Likewise, make each university publish the exact salaries of its top 25 earners, together with what they do (and even which ones fly business class and first class). I can tell you that you would be lucky to find a single professor who publishes and teaches in that list anywhere in Australia. It would be our Vice Chancellors on salaries of over a million dollars per year – so multiples of what a Prime Minister or Chief Justice gets. And then the 'Team' of DVCs, PVCs, Deans of Schools, Heads of Diversity or Equity or whatever it's called that tries for a balance of reproductive organs and skin pigmentation on campus. Let me say this. The bureaucratic and centralised nature of Australian universities simply beggars belief. And the Libs have done nothing about it. Zero. Nada. Nothing. Why? Perhaps because they seem – I have no inside knowledge and can only comment as an observer – to take their advice from sitting VCs.

Then there's the obsession with Grants. This country's universities are obsessed with grants and grant-getting. This is the science model imposed on the rest of the university. To get promoted you need to find someone to give you money to do your research, with the most kudos coming to you if it's the Australian Research Council ('ARC')

– meaning the money comes from the taxpayer. Now let's be blunt. If you're in history, most parts of law, the Arts, much of Business, and big chunks of the rest of the university you can publish in top journals without soliciting a cent of grant money. But then you will never be promoted (and I mean never). The universities have huge grant-getting bureaucracies that need to be fed.

Here is an example I have used various times in the past. Take two academics in the same area who have published in the exact same top line peer-reviewed international journals. Academic A gets no grants. He is, in effect, doing his research on his salary without more taxpayer monies. Academic B, by contrast, gets huge amounts of grant money (providing work for all sorts of university bureaucrats and taking up huge amounts of time in filling out the voluminous trying-for-a-grant paperwork, all of which time is treated as a free good). She produces not a jot more than Academic A. The outputs – the things that ultimately matter – are the same. So how do they fare, comparatively speaking? Academic B, the grant-getter, will be feted and promoted. Academic A, who just publishes without a taxpayer grant, will never, ever get a promotion and may be fired. This is true across Australia. It is bonkers. Universities treat inputs (grant money to allow research to be done) as outputs (what is produced). In fact they care more about the input grants. It is exactly analogous to you choosing to buy your car based on which car company got the most taxpayer support, the most subsidies, the most grants. That is your proxy for excellence. Bonkers, right? (Well, I suppose that actually explains how we buy submarines in this country, but I digress.) Worse, no academic outside Australia judges you based on your grant-getting prowess. They want to know what you've written, and where. Full stop. Again, the Liberals have done nothing about this insanity. And they could fix it without having to pass a Bill through the Senate. This is a Lambie free zone.

And notice that I have thus far been careful not to say a thing about the left-leaning nature of ARC grants in the social sciences. If you favour stopping the boats or Bjorn Lomborg responses to carbon dioxide reduction or a successful plebiscite before changing the definition of marriage (the list goes on and on), you can guess your chances of the ARC giving you grant money. It rhymes with a Roman Emperor. The fifth one. The pyromaniac. Does our governing party, purportedly on the right side of the political spectrum, give a toss about this bias? To ask is to know the answer.

Next there is the lack of competition between universities in this country when it comes to attracting students. Next to no one sends his or her kids away to university. Yet that is largely what happens in my native Canada. And in the United States. And in the UK. And even in New Zealand. So in Canada the University of Toronto has to compete with McGill in Montreal and Queen's in Kingston and UBC in Vancouver for the best students. It has to improve. Ditto everywhere else in the Anglosphere. But not here. Brisbane students stay in Brisbane. I generalise but the best come to UQ. Next best go to QUT. Then to Griffith. And so on down the perceived hierarchy. UQ could be functionally braindead – you understand that that is a conditional hypothetical – and yet we would still get the best students in the State. I doubt that a team of Nobel Prize winners could figure out how to change this. And it applies to Sydney, and Melbourne, everywhere because there is no cross-country competition in this country, competition between G8 unis such as the University of Sydney and Melbourne and UQ. Why? Almost no one leaves home to go to university so any competition is intra-city. Basically it doesn't exist, save for a bit of the intra-city sort between Sydney and UNSW and between Melbourne and Monash. Of course this is not a problem if you don't believe in competition and its powers to produce good outcomes. It is a problem, though, if you believe competition is a force for good.

Penultimately I'll just say a quick word on the rankings of universities that our million dollar a year VCs like to tout. Believe me, these rankings are worthless, meaningless fluff for 99 percent of all questions related to universities. They are focused only on the natural sciences. They have nothing really to say about undergraduate life and teaching (indeed a university's ranking probably goes up if its top professor has been able to win a grant to buy out his teaching responsibilities and so never again sees an undergraduate student). They use criteria such as surveys by others of your perceived prestige, the number of international students and the 'number of Nobel Prize winners on staff' – the last of these literally implying that a university could go out and hire a Nobel laureate, put her up in a five star hotel drinking champagne all year, and its ranking would go up, and by a lot! These rankings say nothing at all about picking a university for an undergraduate – and it is here where Australian unis are particularly awful. Moreover, the rankings criteria seem almost to have been chosen specifically to stop 48 of the world's top 50 universities from being US ones, when in fact they are. (And believe me, as a native born Canadian I do not say this lightly or delightedly.) Put Oxford and Cambridge in the mix near the very top and the other 48 are US universities. See where academics go. See where the money is.

Lastly, I suppose the 'diversity' or 'equity' bureaucracies are worth a quick mention. These are highly paid university bureaucrats whose goal is to get a statistical match between a percentage of something you find in the population at large and what you find across the professoriate or across the student body of the university. Of course the 'diversity' that is being aimed at is one typically focused on the type of reproductive organs you bring to the table, or the type of skin pigmentation you have, or the distant ancestry you can claim (plausibly or implausibly). Now I am opposed to all forms of affirmative action but if the aim is diversity at a university maybe the place to start is with a diversity of political outlooks in the Arts and Social Sciences and Law. Forget it. Australian universities lean massively to the left.

Do Universities Lean Left Politically?

'Prove it Allan', I hear more than a few ABC types proclaim. Okay, then consider this. A few years ago Professor John McGinnis in the United States, with a colleague, examined the political donations of US law school professors at Ivy League universities. Such donations are public information in the US. These ran at over 6:1 flowing to the Democrats over the Republicans. This sort of study showing a significant bias to the left-side of politics has been shown repeatedly in the US. And notice that the 6:1 slant to the left measures only people who give money to political parties. If you think those on the right are more likely to give money and make campaign contributions, the imbalance is worse. Again, notice that the McGinnis study looks at the most elite law schools in the US. Many suppose that the bias or imbalance is worse – and by worse I mean the percentage of conservatives is lower, which is not what some left-wing academics would mean by worse – but it's worse in lesser law schools, because if you're going to tough it out as a Tory/Republican/'Raving-Right-Winger' (to use the accepted academic *mot juste*) you're more likely to do so at Harvard than at the University of Vermont, or Hawaii. Whatever your take on those suppositions, Professor Amy Wax, when reviewing Professor Charles Murray's book *Coming Apart: The State of White America 1960-2010*, describes the vast preponderance of US academics as having 'progressive and liberal commitments'. And bear in mind that the ratio and absolute number of conservatives to lefties will be much, much lower in some disciplines compared to what they are in law. Think gender studies departments. Think critical race theory. Think of much of the social sciences. Or take political science departments. Or take so-called 'social psychologists'. Jon Haidt in the US (a centrist-lefty but unhappy with these results) says his data indicates 96 percent of social psychologists see themselves as left of centre; 3.7 percent as centrists; and (wait for it) 0.3 percent as right of centre. That sort of 'balance' might even make the ABC look good.

Of course that is just the United States. If I had more space I'd also point out that on that campaign donations information for US law schools 91 percent of the Harvard faculty give to the Democrats; 92 percent at Yale; 94 percent at Stanford; and on and on. And here in Australia? Well, after 11 years in this country my opinion, as far as law schools go, is that the skew or imbalance or bias to the left is at least as bad here, probably worse. That earlier-mentioned John McGinnis US left-leaning 6:1 bias or split means that at my university law school you would need to identify about 6 Coalition voters on the academic law school staff out of the 40 or so. Three years ago you could have done that, just. But we've had two retirements. Now, I'm not at all sure. And just to put this in context for you, the UQ law school where I work is widely perceived to be the most right-wing law school in Australia. That means, just to be perfectly clear for you, that my law school gets the label or description of being this country's bastion of right-wingery on the basis that for every one Coalition voter who works in the place there are six voters for left-wing parties. By the way, my own personal belief is also that that 6:1 ratio would be worse, would be more left-leaning, at every other law school in this country – certainly at every one of the big city, best-known universities. Yes, there will be a tax lawyer here and a corporations lawyer there who quietly votes right in the secrecy of the ballot box, but not many. And in public law, my area that deals with such topics as constitutions and so encompasses stopping the boats and getting a bill of rights, those with right of centre political views are very, very rare. As for non-law subjects, there will be disciplines that some might suppose are not likely to add much if any value to a student's life, and in these, well, you might struggle to find any professors who vote right and admit to doing so. Think women's studies, indigenous studies, parts of sociology. And for what it's worth I think the 'left over right' bias in the university sector is worse in Canada than here in Australia, and maybe a tiny bit better in the UK, but maybe not. All that said, there are parts of the universities where political imbalance is not noticed and not nearly as marked. Think engineering, the really hard natural sciences, and perhaps medicine.

Notice as well that the bias or imbalance (the figures are again from the US) has gotten worse over time. A UCLA professor doing work in this area recently claimed that 'the ratio of Democrats to Republicans or Liberals to Conservatives' went from 1:1 in the 1920s to 2:1 in the 1950s to 14:1 in 2010 and it's even worse now. Other empirical work shows the ratio getting more and more skewed since the 1980s. But rest comfortably. No doubt all those lefties who are teaching your kids at university are following former ABC Managing Director Mark Scott's advice (when bias at the ABC was pointed out) and looking inside themselves and presenting their political science lectures in a wholly impartial, balanced and neutral way. Just like the producers and presenters on the main ABC current affairs TV shows, right?

So why is it that there are so few right-of-centre academics? This is a question that gets a lot of speculation thrown its way in the US, though less so here. Four explanations or theories have been put forward.

a)   Brainpower – The claim here is that conservatives aren't as smart. So they can't get jobs in universities. The claim is statistical you understand. It's always possible that the odd bright and intelligent right winger might wander along. But on this theory don't hold your breath. The point here is that there is an imbalance because right-of-centre people aren't qualified; they're too dumb, to work in universities.

b)   Interest – The claim this time is that right wing people aren't interested in working in universities. They want to be out there running some hedge fund or working in banking on Canary Wharf making squillions of dollars to indulge their essentially greedy natures. (I editorialise to make explicit an implicit theme the left tries to disguise.) The point here is that right-of-centre people just aren't interested in working in universities. They have other interests and avenues to pursue. Probably they want to take their law degrees and go work in a big national law firm then become senior partner or maybe switch to the Bar, and either way make dollops of dosh.

c)   Greed – I foreshadowed this claim already, and truth be told it's partly linked with the 'interest' hypothesis. Conservatives, goes this theory, want to make money more than the tree-hugging, social justice warriors on the left (again, I editorialise) and so they have little inclination to work in universities. They are more greedy than those on the left and so university life is correspondingly less attractive. (And if they're not more greedy, well, they're probably in the army shooting guns.)

d)   Discrimination – The claim here is that as the Left today runs the universities it does not go out of its way to hire those on the right. Put bluntly, it discriminates (mostly in indirect ways, but also in terms of what is seen as acceptable research so in that sense in more direct ways too).

So which of these four is it? Well interestingly, Professor James Phillips recently uploaded a new paper of his online, which will soon be published in the *Harvard Journal of Law & Public Policy*. He evaluated all four of these explanations by looking at citation and publication rates of law professors at the top 16 US law schools (focused, as it was, on the law). You can find a nice synopsis of this in the online archives of *The Washington Post*. As I said, Professor Phillips was evaluating these four possible explanations for the apparent lack of law professors with conservative and libertarian views. Guess what he found? First off, those who lean to the right (few in number though they are) are cited more per person and publish more than their peers. Oh, and they tend to have more qualifications than their peers. In fact his data (after regression analysis, propensity score matching and reweighting, nearest neighbour matching and coarsened exact matching) suggested the clear explanation for the lack of conservatives was discrimination. The Left runs the universities and discriminates against those on the right. All you readers will no doubt be shocked – shocked I say – by this revelation.

Back to Universities and Law Schools

Returning to the bureaucratic nature of our law schools, I have discussed the obsession with getting grants, which for most law profs at least – leave aside pragmatic considerations related to trying for promotion – is a complete waste of time. Then there are government mandated 'let's try to measure the quality of the research' exercises. In Canada and the US such comparisons are done by private magazines to sell to would-be students; they're based on woolly assumptions and weird criteria; and they end up producing an ordinal ranking of universities and of law schools. But at least it costs the taxpayers nothing. In this country there is a bureaucratic 'research assessment' exercise that I believe – having made the mistake of being an assessor in the first round when the scheme was initially introduced – produces wholly meaningless data. Gobble-de-gook. If anything it is worse than the North American results. The difference is that Australia's is a government-mandated, bureaucratic scheme that costs tens of millions of dollars (not counting the huge costs of treating academics' time in helping with this nonsense as a free good). In a sense it doesn't even assess individuals while still purporting to give a judgement on research excellence.

There have also been attempted rankings of academic journals

– listed in various quality categories – that have produced laughable results. And soon they are going to try to 'measure' an academic's 'impact'. The thing you need to realise when it comes to Australian universities is that meaningless data is much preferred over no data, as people can be employed to work with meaningless data (and where the results they concoct often can do harm while pretending to do good).

And leave all that aside and turn to teaching. Our universities are so centralised that professors, including law professors, get told how much we must assess students. I am under immense pressure to record my lectures, as is the case widely across the country. Why? Because so many of our law students work. They are supposedly doing a full time degree and yet they work downtown in law offices three, even four days a week. That is a core reason why the expectations for our law students are way, way lower than what they are in Canada, the US and Britain where being a full time student actually means – wait for it – being a full time student (with maybe a bartending job one night a week). Not here. The inevitable result is that our expectations in Aussie law schools are lower than they are in other Anglosphere countries' law schools. You can't read as much when you're a student working 3 or 4 days a week at a big law firm. I suppose I could ask for a grant to try to prove that, but would it be a good use of taxpayers' money? Oh, and the lowered expectations go hand-in-hand with pretty massive grade inflation! I have seen it in just my eleven years in working at a university in this country. Yesterday's C is today's B, or higher.

Then there is the fact we have so many law schools for the size of the country. It was 42 or 43 law schools at last count, though if you go to sleep the number can go up on you – and 13 in NSW alone! To put that in context, in English Canada (so that's about 27 million people or so) there are 17 law schools. Most take only 150 to 180 students per year. Here in Australia we have QUT and Monash taking in, what, over a thousand students each a year. In fact per capita we now turn out more law students than the US. Wow! Hands up if you think that is the way to achieve the Turnbullian 'innovation' revolution dream – by flooding the country with lawyers.

So we have too many law schools, taking in too many students each, and allowing students basically to be working near-on full time while supposedly studying full time (by listening to recorded lectures each night and by the university's keeping expectations way down and grades way up). And these law schools all exist in a wider university that is massively too centralised, too regulated, too one-size-fits-all, and too top down. In addition, we are also supposed to pretend that all the law schools in the country are more or less equal. Of course that is simply untrue. Some are awful. In my opinion, even the best law schools in Australia are not as good as Otago law school in New Zealand, and certainly nowhere near as good as the best ones in Britain, the US or even Canada.

Concluding Remarks

Some might say this discussion has failed to tackle the really big picture stuff, such as the need to bring in more realistic (ie higher) student tuition fees – which I support. Or omitting to discuss ways in which incentives should be put in place so that universities have some sort of stake or skin in the game in seeing that students pay back their loans – which I also support. But those issues can be attacked while also attempting to reform all of the problems discussed above, which would be easier to accomplish, not least because many of them would win support from academics across the political spectrum who are overwhelmingly sick of the managerial, bureaucratic, one-size-fits-all nature of Australian universities. Readers might have thought that a right-of-centre government that actually did believe in small government and taxpayer value for money – to say nothing of one that wanted even a modicum of political balance in its tertiary education sector – could do something about some of the above-discussed problems. Alas, this post-2013 Liberal government has (or if you see the Turnbull incarnation as a separate beast then 'these post-2013 Liberal governments have') done nothing. The Libs have been a huge disappointment, to me at least, on the tertiary education front.

Aboriginal Australia

Kerryn Pholi

Author, writer and researcher in Indigenous policy and affairs

As a relative newcomer to your side of politics, I feel a little presumptuous to be talking to you about where the Right should be headed when it comes to Aboriginal affairs. Who am I to be telling you what to think, or say, or do?

The thing I like most about you people on the Right is that you *don't* need me to tell you what to think about Aboriginal issues. You don't timidly wait to hear my opinion before expressing your own, and you don't scramble to adjust your opinion to better agree with mine. You know your own values, and you aren't going to dissemble or compromise simply because I can lay claim to an Aboriginal identity and you can't. You understand that Aboriginality alone does not equate to wisdom, and you expect as much clarity of thought and sound reasoning from me as you would from any other contributor in this book.

That's you at your best, at any rate. The debate over Aboriginal affairs is particularly fraught and conflicted, and we are all only human. When you are surrounded by well-meaning woolly-mindedness and mysticism, you can easily begin to doubt your own reasoning. When the terrain is mined with exquisite sensitivities and obscure protocols, it is tempting to surrender the field to the

Aboriginal players and leave them to it – because after all, it's not really any of your business, is it? One could reasonably conclude that, if a nonsense gesture, a trivial compromise, a gap in logic or a relaxation of reasoning makes Aboriginal people happy, then surely it would be churlish to object.

I would argue that Aboriginal people deserve better than that from you, and that we need you, the Right, at your best.

The most popular self-help books are the ones that affirm the things you already know. That's all I can aim to do here, because I hold no secret, special Aboriginal knowledge that I can impart; all that mystical 'Indigenous knowings' nonsense is just another identity-politics power play. But you already knew that, didn't you?

Where is Aboriginal Australia heading?

I'm not here to dispense wisdom on how Aboriginal people feel, on what Aboriginal people really want, or on what they need in order to 'close the gap'. Given that many (but not all) Aboriginal people dislike the things I say, my views on such matters could hardly be considered representative. However, if we are here to talk about what you, the Right, should be doing about Aboriginal affairs, we should establish some context on where Aboriginal Australia is at and where it is heading.

A growing 'Aboriginal' population

Generations of intermarriage and an increased propensity for Australians of mixed heritage to self-identify as Aboriginal has produced the rapid growth of a geographically, economically and socially diverse Aboriginal population. This diversity, which encompasses a sizable Aboriginal middle class who are virtually indistinguishable in appearance and behaviour from their non-Aboriginal neighbours, makes the framing of Aboriginal people as a homogenously disadvantaged group increasingly hard to sustain. Despite this demographic shift, the exclusive entitlements, exceptions, structures and services that were established to resolve Aboriginal disadvantage remain in place and are largely unexamined. As is the case with any affirmative action policy approach, the urbanised, integrated, middle-class Aboriginal population is best positioned to take advantage of these measures, both as direct beneficiaries and as career administrators in the institutions and sectors where such special measures are able to flourish. This influential class of Aboriginal administrators and beneficiaries is deeply invested in maintaining a narrative of ubiquitous Aboriginal disadvantage, and in promoting separatism over integration as the preferred solution.

A visible, dysfunctional, 'white' underclass

Meanwhile, in Australia and other developed nations we are seeing a growing underclass with roots in intergenerational welfare dependency, and with social problems of a nature and scale to rival those of remote and marginalised Aboriginal communities. The presence of this non-Aboriginal underclass and its attendant problems in Australia makes it harder to convincingly attribute entrenched disadvantage in some Aboriginal communities to the effects of 'colonisation' or 'Stolen Generations'.

Competing ethnicities

We are also seeing visible changes in Australia's ethnic make-up. While teaching at TAFE, a number of Sudanese students in my introductory legal studies class were curious about the function of

'Koori Courts' and other Aboriginal-specific mechanisms. *"We are tribal people too"* they said. *"We are displaced, and our communities are troubled, like the Aboriginal people. And we too are black people! So where are our special courts, our special laws, and our special services?"* An influx of migrants and refugees representing the global nature of extreme human suffering undermines the cogency of Aboriginal Australia's claim to a unique and unrivalled grievance.

Competing identities

As the urban, integrated Aboriginal population continues to grow, there is potential for Aboriginality alone to diminish in status as a distinct indicator of a marginalised identity group, as it simply won't be all that special anymore. In addition, a range of identity groups are now competing for recognition of their marginalisation, disadvantage and historical suffering. Socially progressive corporations and institutions, weary of supporting the unrewarding Reconciliation agenda, may be more inclined to direct their resources toward more appealing and responsive causes, such as LGBTI rights.

The Aboriginal industry has not yet been affected by the 'intersectionality' trend that has divided other movements into ever-diminishing, fractious sub-groups defined by gender identification, sexual preference, physical and psychological conditions and various combinations thereof. How has the Aboriginal industry maintained cohesion when all around are succumbing to the narcissism of small differences? Perhaps because there is more to be gained from an appearance of solidarity than from engaging in intellectual squabbles that could draw unwanted attention to the chasm of difference between the integrated Aboriginal middle-class and the welfare-dependent Aboriginal underclass.

Generational change

The renewed urgency surrounding calls for constitutional recognition and treaties can be attributed, at least in part, to an ageing Aboriginal political vanguard that is now shifting into legacy mode. The activists of the 1970s and 80s became the elder statesmen (and a few women) of today, and many would like to see some reward for their efforts before handing the reins to the next generation.

And who will take their place? The younger of the Aboriginal political class has been nurtured and tutored by beneficial programs and benevolent institutions. As a result, they are polished and articulate, but have little experience or understanding of genuine political battle. They have had no need to mobilise, organise and agitate in pursuit of their goals, as there are few Aboriginal battles left for young activists to cut their teeth upon. Aboriginal issues – such as remote community development, anti-racism, violence and incarceration rates, closing the gap, constitutional recognition and the demand for a treaty – have for quite some time been the business of government departments and well-funded NGOs. This generation of emerging Aboriginal leaders perceives no conflict between their political convictions and their professional roles in the state-sponsored Aboriginal industry. Their ability to defend their convictions and justify their roles against substantial and substantiated critique has not yet been tested.

Reconciliation fatigue

The latest crop of young Australians entering the workforce are well-versed in the edicts of Aboriginal Reconciliation, having grown up with routine 'Welcome to Country' ceremonies, annual Sorry Days, and multiple viewings of 'Rabbit Proof Fence'. While this generation might have received more knowledge of Aboriginal culture and history (or a particular version of it, at any rate) than previous generations, they may turn out to be less inclined to regard Aboriginal people as tragically disadvantaged victims. Younger Australians have grown accustomed to the presence of Aboriginal interests in the governance of their schools, sporting groups, universities and workplaces. Rather than view Aboriginal people as powerless objects of pity, they recognise the Aboriginal industry as a powerful and influential force. Having been drilled for years in the historical suffering of Aboriginal people at the hands of merciless colonials, young Australians may be somewhat inured to ongoing Aboriginal suffering at the hands of other Aboriginal people. I suspect many young people are sceptical and bored with the entire Reconciliation project, but they have been well-schooled in the art of feigning respectful interest.

The direction in which Aboriginal Australia is heading presents interesting opportunities for the Right to exert some influence. Of course, there is a significant element that will always strive to stand in your way. We could *kvetch* forever about the myriad irritations and frustrations the Left present, but in the spirit of self-help I have instead focussed on three key areas where the Right hold an advantage that can be put to good use in influencing the future of Aboriginal Australia.

Right vs Left: Three themes

Guilt

Many on the Left in this country are living with a chronic case of middle-class guilt. A keen anxiety around Aboriginal disadvantage offers both an explanation for, and a means to displace, this vaguely unpleasant feeling. It seems far more noble to feel a sense of guilt that your presence has displaced and disrupted 'the oldest living culture' than it does to feel guilty about simply living a prosperous and healthy life in a beautiful country. Similarly, many well-meaning folk are supportive of Aboriginal claims for specific rights and concessions 'because Aboriginal people haven't had the same privileges as the rest of us.' If you are inclined to feel guilty anyway, it seems better to feel guilt at your good fortune relative to the misfortunes of an abstract Aboriginal 'other' than to foolishly feel guilty about nothing you can quite put your finger on.

In contrast, the Right are refreshingly, cheerfully free of any such guilt – or at least, that's how you appear to me. The problem, as I see it, is the way you respond to the Left's self-flagellation. You either drive yourselves half-mad with frustration trying to reason the Left out of their middle-class angst, or you simply dismiss their feelings of guilt around Aboriginal issues as trivial and self-indulgent. Regardless of whether we believe the Left's sense of guilt is warranted or worthwhile, we would do well to acknowledge that these feelings are genuinely held if we are to have a constructive debate with our friends on the Left on Aboriginal issues.

Modernity

Dissatisfaction with modernity and a fascination with experimental economies makes remote Aboriginal Australia an endlessly attractive diversion for the Left. Remote Aboriginal Australia is far away and enigmatic; a mute and picturesque screen on which to project a fantasy of a more spiritual, authentic, innocent lifestyle. Many of my colleagues in Aboriginal affairs were earnest, sensitive women with degrees in humanities and the arts; one trip to the Garma Festival or a whistle-stop 'stakeholder engagement' tour of remote communities, and they would be hooked on the notion that it was both possible and desirable to preserve the remote Aboriginal lifestyle.

One colleague explained to me that she wanted her work to ensure that 'something different to the whitefella world' was maintained 'out there somewhere'. When I pointed out that she and her children had benefitted greatly from the education and opportunities offered by this 'whitefella world', she protested that she herself had not enjoyed school very much, whereas the children in remote communities enjoyed an enviable degree of freedom. I then asked whether she would have preferred that her own children received the standard of education offered in remote communities, instead of the standard offered by the private school they currently attended. My colleague wistfully replied that even though her own children were regrettably growing up in a modern, 'white' world that deprived them of authentic spiritual experiences and a deep connection with nature, she drew comfort from the fact that some Aboriginal children still had the opportunity to grow up immersed in their own natural, spiritual culture.

The Left dreams of a system that allows Aboriginal people to opt out of modernity, because then there may be hope that they too could sidestep its tiresome demands. Aboriginal leaders cannily nurture the fantasy:

> *"What Aboriginal people ask is that the modern world now makes the sacrifices necessary to give us a real future. To relax its grip on us. To let us breathe, to let us be free of the determined control exerted on us to make us like you...."* Galarrwuy Yunupingu, 'The Monthly', June 2016.

In general, the Right holds more expert understanding of how economies actually work, and is therefore well-positioned to rigorously scrutinise the Left's notions for experimental economies in remote Aboriginal communities. While there is nothing wrong with theorising alternative economic and social orders, the Left must be continuously reminded that Aboriginal Australia is not their own private petri dish.

Responsibility

The Left and the Right hear different things when the word 'responsibility' is spoken. The Left connotes 'responsibility' with abandoning the vulnerable, blaming the victim, and absolving the villain. They will argue, for example, that the poor should not be expected to take responsibility for themselves when the rich are responsible for creating inequality. They will claim that Aboriginal people should not be expected to take responsibility for their present circumstances, because their historical victimisation negates any such obligation. The Left perceives 'responsibility' in negative terms of blame and culpability, and sees the allocation of responsibility as a binary system: the villain bears all, the victim bears none.

The Right has an entirely different relationship to the concept of responsibility. Rather than view it as a burden, the Right finds far more joy in responsibility, and in the autonomy it fosters, than discomfort. The Right views 'responsibility' in positive terms of agency, empowerment and self-respect, and finds it hard to understand why the Left would wish to obstruct Aboriginal people's access to these rewards.

While these struggles over meaning are played out around them, many Aboriginal people feel that both the Left and the Right fail to grasp the realities of their lives. The Left regards Aboriginal culture as something blessed and almost otherworldly, to be revived and preserved, and wishes to foster Aboriginal people in their designated roles as cultural custodians. The Right has a more realistic view of traditional Aboriginal culture as something meaningful to Aboriginal people but largely incompatible with modernity, and is more inclined to view Aboriginal people as human beings first and culture-bearers second. The Right also more readily acknowledges that integration and self-reliance, rather than continued separatism and dependence on the state, is the way forward. However, it does sometimes seem that the Right does not fully understand, let alone empathise with, the pain and loss that marks the transition from a lifelong state of infantilisation to one of personal responsibility and autonomy.

Where to from here?

Beyond 'You need to take responsibility'

Personal responsibility is an acquired taste. For those of us who had little exposure to the concept in our formative years, it is a difficult practice to develop in later life. Whereas if you were raised to maintain a sense of personal responsibility as habitually as oral hygiene and saying 'please' and 'thank you', it may be hard for you to understand why some people find the concept so threatening.

The Right takes pride in its emphasis on personal responsibility, but would do well to speak more openly about the challenges, the rewards, and the practical steps towards getting there. The Left will sneer and dismiss you as 'patronising', but these are the stories that some of us need to hear. If the Right want to see Aboriginal people take more responsibility, you need to be prepared to explain precisely what 'taking responsibility' looks like and how it is to be done.

Disenfranchised Aboriginal people won't be persuaded to make dramatic and difficult changes in the way they live simply through being hectored to pull their socks up and take responsibility. They need to see a point in joining the modernity project, and they need to see a place for themselves within it. The aspirations of many Aboriginal people are aligned with the values of the Right: a desire for autonomy, and a desire to minimise the intrusion of governments in our lives; satisfaction in the dignity of work and in generating our own incomes; finding pride in our conduct and our capacities as individuals, rather than simply 'being proud' of being Aboriginal. These alignments should be pointed out at every opportunity. The

Right's engagement with Aboriginal Australia should be approached not as a rescue mission, but as a recruitment drive.

Reclaiming the language

The Left have long held the rhetorical advantage in Aboriginal political debate. The Left has had an easier time of promoting emotionally-laden and vaguely defined concepts like 'reconciliation' and 'recognition' than the Right has had of promoting its dry principles of personal responsibility, integration, minimal state intervention and so on. Yet the indefinite terms floated by the Left could easily break up upon the rocks of the realistic and pragmatic Right, if the wind were to change just a little. Instead of setting out to argue endlessly with the Left over whether an idea like 'recognition' is right or wrong, or whether or not a policy is 'assimilationist', it may sometimes be more effective to simply invite them to explain precisely what they *mean* when they use these terms. If we are tired of the Left dismissing all scepticism and protest as 'racism', we must first insist on a clear explanation of precisely how the term 'racism' is applicable in each instance. Taking the bait lends legitimacy to the Left's irresponsible and lazy use of language. Make them work for it instead.

The Left also have a long tradition of policing speech for the slightest hint of insensitivity or chauvinism. The Right can play that game equally well by emphasising the plurality of Aboriginal society. When the Left speaks of Aboriginal rights, for instance, ask *whose rights* are they talking about specifically. Do they speak of the rights of Aboriginal women and children living under the remnants of traditional customs in remote communities, or the rights of the powerful community leaders and their families, whose interests dominate these communities? Is the Left speaking of the rights of Aboriginal welfare recipients, or of Aboriginal organisations, or the rights of Aboriginal taxpayers? When the Left talks about Aboriginal people, they should always be asked to explain who, precisely, they are talking about.

Claim the future – and let the Left have the past

While I suggested earlier that the Right should acknowledge the reality of the Left's guilty feelings, that was not to suggest that these sentiments should be indulged. It cannot be emphasised enough that middle class guilt, 'white privilege' guilt, and postcolonial 'settler shame' are pointless, selfish and a waste of everybody's time.

An acquaintance of mine once suggested that a successful and prosperous person such as he would have no understanding of the Aboriginal 'lived experience', and should therefore respectfully refrain from offering opinions or intruding upon Aboriginal people's processes for solving their own problems. This is palpable nonsense. The more prosperous and privileged you are, the more skills, knowledge and resources you have to offer. A protestation of guilt is simply a genteel means of ducking one's responsibilities as a citizen. Remind your dithering friends that if they genuinely care about Aboriginal futures, they have a duty to share what they know and believe, not an obligation to withhold it. The perception of Aboriginal people as mute and passive victims has led the broader community to forget that Aboriginal people are perfectly capable of telling you where to go if they don't want to hear your opinion.

Despite the best efforts of serious historians, the Left will continue to say what they will about Australia's ghastly history of systematic Aboriginal persecution. Leave them to wallow in their shame; their attachment to the past forbids them from setting out a vision for an Aboriginal future. They believe it is 'oppressive' to 'dictate' to Aboriginal people how they should live or what their goals should be. The Right should have no such compunction, and can buoyantly say to Aboriginal Australia, 'We are heading in this direction, and we want to bring you with us'.

Talking about the future means talking about children. The Right can reclaim the language and reframe the debate where it matters most by talking about Aboriginal children as *Australian* children, as *our* citizens of the future. Instead of allowing the debate to be framed in terms of the problems and needs of 'Aboriginal communities', we must continually drag the focus back to the needs of the children *within* these communities. The abstract 'needs' of a community cannot take precedence over the tangible needs of its own children, and children must not be sacrificed in service to an idea of 'community' or 'culture'.

The Left likes to characterise the Right as made up of 'rich white men'. So be it – there is no better way for the Right to demonstrate its values than for these so-called 'rich white men' to invest in the protection of vulnerable Aboriginal children, and to reclaim a stake in the future of Aboriginal Australia.

Health - Opt-Out of Medicare and Opt-In for Personal Health Savings Accounts

Jeremy Sammut

Senior Research Fellow & Director of Health Innovations Program
at The Centre for Independent Studies

The Politics of Medicare: 1990-2016

The perception the Labor Party's successful 'Mediscare' was an important factor contributing to the loss of support for the Turnbull government during the 2016 federal election – especially among pensioner and retired voters that traditionally support the Coalition – has reinforced the belief that health is the third-rail of Australian politics. The conventional wisdom that Medicare is an untouchable political sacred cow means that initiating a feasible health reform agenda depends, primarily, on discovering a politically viable health policy – a policy capable of running the electoral gauntlet and winning the popular consent and approval of the Australian people at an election. If the Right is to understand what it might take to achieve health reform, it is vital, in the first instance, to understand how the politics of health have played out over the last quarter of a century, so that sound health policy development is informed and underpinned by an equally effective political strategy.

During the eight-week election campaign, Labor exploited a relatively minor administrative matter – the outsourcing to the private sector of Medicare's claims processing system – to allege that the future of a 'free' and universal tax-payer funded health system rested on the outcome of the poll. While overdrawn – the Coalition, as far as is discernible, has no coherent policy alternative to Medicare at present – the health-focused attack on the government should have been anticipated and responded to more effectively by the Prime Minister, Malcolm Turnbull, and by Health Minister, Sussan Ley. Since Bob Hawke's fourth and final election victory in 1990, Labor has only won two federal elections in its own right. Each victory – the 1993 GST election and the 2007 Work Choices election – was on the back of Labor campaigning hard on bread and butter issues. Health played a role in each victory as well. The health proposals of opposition leader John Hewson featured heavily in Labor's attack on the *Fightback* economic reform blueprint in 1993 when the Coalition lost the 'unloseable' election. And Kevin Rudd's victory in 2007 was in part attributable to his (subsequently unfulfilled) promise to fix Medicare by ending the blame game over health between the Commonwealth and the States.

The lesson taught by the last quarter of a century seems to be that Labor does well electorally when it fights on its traditional territory – the core economic and social policies that define the relationship between government and voters. This was the political lesson that John Howard learned during the course of his prime ministership. After proposing in the early-2000s some modest changes to Medicare to expand the role of private insurance, by the mid-2000s the Howard government struck upon a signature slogan designed to eliminate health as a vote-swinging issue. The Howard government went to the polls in 2004 describing the Coalition as "the best friend Medicare has ever had", on the back of initiatives introduced by health minister Tony Abbott to boost the rate of bulk billing and defuse Labor's attack over the small decline that had occurred in the proportion of 'free' GP visits.

Health and the Commanding Heights of Government

Prime Minister Turnbull tried to emulate the Howard approach and neutralise Labor's scare tactic by promising that Medicare was a vital government service which the Coalition would 'never ever' privatise. But the message appears to have struggled to cut through, a failing probably attributable to the lacklustre "Team Turnbull" election campaign in general. There are suggestions that the Prime Minister should have lived up to his promise when he announced his leadership challenge to then Prime Minister Tony Abbott in September 2015, that if victorious he would provide economic leadership and build consensus for change by explaining the need for reform in the national interest. However, the temptation to hoist the Prime Minister by his own words is too harsh, not only given the Howard precedent, but also given the evidence – the election results in 1993 and 2007 – that 'dry' health and other policies leave the Coalition especially vulnerable to being wedged electorally.

The political wisdom of treating health as a special case and uncoupling the issue from the theme of economic reform is also supported by overseas experience. In the 1980s in the United Kingdom, the Tory government led by Margaret Thatcher privatised the commanding heights of the economy by implementing free market policies including the de-nationalisation of industry. But the Thatcher government left the socialist National Health System untouched by major reform, and never dared to suggest that British voters should cease to consume healthcare without charge at point of access paid for by taxes. Thatcher (much like Howard's view of Medicare 20 years later) judged that health was a settled political question, in the sense that the majority of voters supported the status quo, to the point that tampering with the NHS would place the Tories in mortal electoral peril.

No Australian government, moreover, not even during the widely praised era of reform in the 1980s and 1990s under the Hawke-Keating and Howard-Costello governments, has ever sought re-election by running on an explicitly 'economic rationalist' platform, let alone in the specific area of health. In addition, an unwillingness to pledge to undertake significant health reform hardly makes the Turnbull government unique compared to contemporary conservative governments in other comparable nations. In all western democracies, the largest and fastest growing areas of government – public health, state education, and social welfare systems – are in need of reform to rein in government spending: the problem is that no western politician knows how to undertake the necessary reforms to scale back unsustainable entitlement programs and get re-elected. Health, together with education and welfare, remain the commanding heights of government – issues that can make or break the victory or defeat of governments at the ballot box.

To be fair as well, Turnbull's problems in health were exacerbated by, and illustrated by, the fate of the Abbott government's health policy. After having disastrously promised there would be no cuts to health, education or the ABC at the eleventh hour of the 2013 election campaign, the Abbott government announced as part of the 2014 budget a $7 Medicare co-payment in order to recoup some of the cost of health directly from users and contribute to budget repair. The Medicare co-payment was eventually abandoned – it was "dead, buried, and cremated" said Abbott to underline his mistake and apologise to the Australian people – mainly in response to the political backlash that was orchestrated by the organised medical profession through the offices of the Australian Medical Association (AMA).

The political fallout from co-payment policy contributed to the momentum within the federal parliamentary Liberal Party for a leadership change. Hence, there is little mystery why the Turnbull government was never going to play to Labor's strengths and campaign for re-election on a health reform platform. Nevertheless, the fresh memory of the Abbott co-payment (in combination with the Turnbull government's commitment to the replacement saving measure – the Medicare rebate freeze) almost certainly enhanced the success of Labor's Mediscare by giving credence to the otherwise unfounded claim that the Coalition would look favourably on major changes to Medicare.

Lessons of the Co-Payment Debacle

The political message of the last three years appears to be that the Coalition would be wise to leave Medicare well enough alone. Yet the way forward for the Right in health is indicated by the contrary political lessons that can be learned from the Medicare co-payment debacle to inform a politically viable approach to health reform. The chief lesson is that making health all about cuts and savings to balance the government's books is a strategic error, counter-productive, and a political dead end. The focus should instead be on exploring innovative ways to give people a superior alternative to the compulsory Medicare scheme that will allow individuals to take back control of the taxes that fund the public health system. Australians should be given the opportunity to save and spend their own health dollars more wisely and efficiently to pay for their own healthcare by establishing an opt-in system of personal health savings accounts. The Right needs to get behind the 'opt-out of Medicare' proposal devised in 2014 by The Centre for Independent Studies' Health Innovations Program, which is consistent with core conservative principles of choice, personal responsibility, and private and market solutions for public policy problems – including the pressing issue of the ever-escalating costs of Medicare.

Public health expenditure is continuing to increase at rates higher than growth in national income. Over the last decade, health is the area of government responsibility which has placed greatest pressure on the federal budget, and thus exacerbated the problem of increasing budget deficits and public debt. As a result, much of the discussion of health policy is centred around exploring ways to bend the cost curve down and limit the impact on the public finances. This discussion has been conducted with a view to long-term health system sustainability in coming decades given the challenges posed by Australia's ageing population, and has been framed by the periodic release by the Federal Treasury of the Intergenerational Reports, which project the impact of current policy settings on the federal budget over the next 40 years.

The fourth Intergenerational Report was released by the Abbott government in March 2015 and delivered the same message as the previous three IGRs by outlining how ageing combined with new medical technology would drive up government health spending and make Medicare unaffordable without imposing significant tax hikes on future generations. Yet in terms of generating momentum for health reform, IGR4 (like its predecessors) has sunk without a trace. The theme of long-term affordability – together with intergenerational fairness and the risk of diminished access to services – simply has not gained traction as a stimulus for reform, despite how vital the fiscal challenges in health are to the availability of private and public resources to pay for other needs and wants.

The reasons why this theme has not gained traction are the same reasons why the attempt to link a small element of cost-sharing, via the Medicare co-payment, to the task of budget repair failed so badly. Rejection of the co-payment was not a symbol of the popular commitment to the "fairness" of the Medicare scheme as presented by the public health lobby. Instead, the rejection was driven by an understandably selfish but rational calculus by middle Australia, which would not accept the clawback of health entitlements for the sake of preventing deficits and debt.

The Labor opposition helped kill the co-payment by describing it as a 'GP Tax' – a phrase that said more than was intended. The co-payment was an easy political kill because Medicare's popularity – among middle and higher income earners – is underwritten by the fact the scheme is one of the most obvious ways that people who feel they pay too much tax get some of their taxes back from government. This is the entitlement mentality in action. But it is also a measure of people who are forced to put so much income into the pot seeking recompense and every opportunity possible to take out as much as possible to get some of their hard-earned back.

In other words, the exercise of the nation's collective social conscience didn't kill the co-payment – the killer factor instead was the flexing of the hip-pocket nerve. On this account, the death of the co-payment can be interpreted as an expression of dissatisfaction with the size of government and the corresponding tax take. The political implications for health reform are crucial. Changes to the health system need, of course, to serve the public interest by creating a sustainable funding mechanism for the sake of the public finances. But the more positive message that emerges from the Medicare co-payment debacle – if you accept its rejection was the rejection of another tax – is that the clear and definable winners out of the health reform process have to be individual voters and taxpayers if change is to be politically feasible.

Anatomy of a Choice-Based Alternative

Average per person total federal, state and territory government spending on health currently sits at around $4500 per annum. This – the 'hidden cost' of Medicare – comes as quite a surprise to ordinary Australians. This figure represents an opportunity to think creatively about health reform and about giving people a choice of alternative ways to pay for and insure their health.

One in every $10 in the economy – or almost 10% of annual GDP or $155 billion per year – is spent on health. Approximately 70% of that money is spent by governments, and approximately 70% of that spending – roughly $70 billion per annum currently – is expended through the three main Medicare programs – the Medical Benefits Scheme (MBS), the Pharmaceutical Benefits Scheme (PBS) and 'free' public hospital care. Medicare basically operates as a set of payments and funding mechanisms that guarantee doctors' incomes, prop up the business model of pharmacists, and protect the wages and conditions of public hospital doctors and nurses. A vocal public lobby of vested interests, backed by public sector health unions and their politician-clients, increases the political challenges associated with health reform.

Railing against vested interests – especially considering the community standing of health professionals – will not get us very far in generating enthusiasm for reform unless we find a way to beat the public choice obstacles to change. This requires reframing the health debate – akin to the way we think about the reform challenge in other areas of the public sector – in terms of releasing the value locked up in the existing highly regimented and captured health system to the individual voters who need to be converted into supporters of health reform.

An elegant solution to the health policy and political conundrum is to allow individuals to opt-out of Medicare. This would involve converting current taxpayer-funded health entitlements that would otherwise fund Medicare into a yearly, indexed 'voucher' for deposit in a superannuation-style, tax-advantaged health savings account (which would attracted the same 15% concessional tax rate as superannuation).

Withdrawals of money deposited in health savings accounts would be permitted to pay for lower cost health services including an approved list of GP visits and other non-hospital care. Health savings accounts are also designed to pay for private health insurance premiums to cover chronic and catastrophic conditions, and thereby meet the high-cost of hospital admissions and major illness, as well as pay for co-payments and deductibles applying to insured services.

Part of the logic behind health savings accounts is that because people are spending their money to purchase more of their own healthcare they will be more cost-conscious consumers of health services, based on the common sense principle that people will always spend their own money more wisely than they spend the government's or a health fund's money. Traditional health systems in countries like Australia that rely heavily on third-party private or public insurance to pay for the bulk of health services are plagued by 'moral hazard' – the problem of over-use and over-servicing leading to a demand and cost spiral attributable to the absence of price signals at the point of consumption.

Gadiel and Sammut (see *Lessons from Singapore: Opt-Out Health Savings Accounts for Australia,* The Centre for Independent Studies'

Policy Monograph 140, July 2014) have shown that Singapore spends a fraction of its national income on health when judged against comparable OECD countries such as Australia (4% of GDP compared to over 9%), while achieving the same or better health outcomes. What sets the design of the cost-effective Singaporean system apart is a national system of income-based, contributory, personal health savings accounts that are used to pay for health services and health insurance, combined with high levels of personal financial accountability for health expenditures through use of prices at point of consumption. This includes extensive use of direct patient charges for out-of-hospital care, complemented by the use of insurance deductibles and co-payments for all inpatient care to directly cost share with patients.

Under the opt-out model proposed for Australia, the incentives to consume health services wisely and affordably would be enhanced by linking personal health savings accounts to individuals' superannuation accounts. If health 'vouchers' ceased upon retirement, and super and health savings accounts were merged upon retirement (as occurs in Singapore), the 'health savings' generated could be used to pay for both old age health costs and to increase retirement incomes. In other words, individuals would benefit financially from this model of health reform, and reap the rewards released by withdrawing from Medicare and assuming personal responsibility for self-funding their own health care.

A New Political Paradigm for Health Reform

Little progress has been made in Australia in dealing with long-term health system sustainability challenges. Ideally, a two-pronged strategy is needed that shifts health costs off government budgets and boosts the efficiency and cost-effectiveness of health services. Pay-As-You Go taxpayer funded health systems like Medicare have always had to ration care because governments cannot afford to pay for all the health care the community wants each year out of the taxes the community is willing to pay. The financially sustainable way to fund modern healthcare, given the demographic and technological realities we face, is to enable people to save up and pay for healthcare over time using an appropriate mix of self-financing and third-party insurance arrangements. Private provision of hospital services also needs to be expanded to address the inefficiencies inherent in cossetted public hospitals, and deliver greater value to the community – more and better healthcare – for our scarce health dollars.

Opt-out health savings accounts would move health policy settings in a direction that would achieve these objectives. By allowing individuals to save and self-finance old age health costs, health system sustainability would be improved by creating significant off-budget sources of health funding. Over time, increasing amounts of health care would be funded by health savings accounts – aided by the magic of compound interest – rather than by taxes, reducing health-related fiscal pressures.

Health savings accounts would also improve overall health system sustainability not only by addressing the problem of moral hazard, but also by creating a contestable market for more efficient provision of insured health services. Health funds – competing for members and seeking to keep premiums low – would operate as price and quality conscious purchasers of hospital services on behalf of members, negotiating service contracts and preferred-provider relationships with public and private hospitals. The need to compete for customers would spur publicly owned-and-operated facilities to boost productivity and emulate the more business-like practices of privately operated competitors. The competition and efficiency effects would be enhanced by the fact that price and quality-conscious consumers – due to the use of co-payments and deductibles – would be spending their own health dollars to access hospital services.

Health savings accounts could also potentially weaken resistance of vested interests opposed to reform. The organised medical profession's opposition to any tampering with Medicare is based on the spectre of 'managed care' impacting adversely on doctors' incomes; this is the fear that private health funds will force doctors to agree to capitation payments – a bulk fee for treating an agreed number of fund members. Health savings accounts, however, would allow for the retention of self-funded, fee-for-service payments and the free choice of doctor for the vast majority of GP and specialist consultations.

This is just one of the political advantages of opt-out health savings accounts. This proposal would create a new political paradigm for health reform predicated on the principle of choice: those who wanted to stay with Medicare would be free to do so and their entitlements would be unaltered. But those who want an alternative would be free to choose. This would represent a health innovation rather than a reform per se – the latter term in health and in other policy areas having acquired a bad name as a synonym for 'losers'. There would be no losers from a voluntary opt-out/opt-in process for establishing health savings accounts, and the great Australian political god of 'fairness' would be satisfied through the retention of Medicare for those who want it. Promoting this simple message – that people are free to stick with Medicare if they wish – would allow the health debate to advance beyond the spectacle of duelling scare and counter-scare campaigns that marred the 2016 election.

The idea of making changes to the health system could be politically detoxified – while respecting the choices of those who want to stay with Medicare – by explicitly likening a voluntary shift to an opt-in saving-based health financing system to school education policy. Opt-out health savings accounts are a natural extension of the market principle of choice that is applied in other areas of public policy to allow people to escape from what otherwise would be compulsory participation in monopolistic public services. Most Australians are comfortable with a choice-based approach to education, which means that government funding is used to support those Australian families who choose not to opt for government schools and wish to send their children to non-government schools. The principle of choice is already applied to health in a limited fashion through the taxpayer-funded PHI Rebate, which supports the cost of the insurance premiums paid by the 45% of Australians who are members of private health funds. The freedom to choose in health would be extended much further if Australians are allowed to opt-out of Medicare.

Based on income, those who opted out would still contribute their taxes to the cost of Medicare, preserving the scheme's redistributive principles. But this does not mean that the low incomed would not look favourably on opting out – the size of the health voucher would make health savings accounts an attractive proposition, further addressing fairness and equity concerns. A likely outcome might be that older groups, naturally, would stick with Medicare – thus preventing the Coalition being wedged on health reform and losing votes among its traditional supporters – while younger groups would be more likely to opt-out. This would amount to an intergenerational transition that resembles the similar transition and the principles of life-time saving that have applied to superannuation and pre-funding of retirement incomes since 1990 – making health savings accounts a more or less familiar and far from radical proposal once explained to the public.

The parallels with superannuation are important for another political reason in terms of building a broader constituency in favour of innovative health reform. Opt-out health savings accounts could win institutional support for change from outside of traditional health care players, given the potential for significant new funds being made available for management by the financial services industry. The political capital and strategic influence the banking and funds management sector could bring to bear from outside of the health system could help reshape the health reform debate and counteract the power of insider health stakeholder groups determined to defend the Medicare status quo.

Beating the Entitlement Trap

If the Australian Right wants to make any headway in health it must find a way to beat at its own game the entitlement mentality trap that helps prop up big government welfare programs like Medicare. No apologies should be made for appealing to the hip pocket nerve and offering people an alternative to Medicare that will be good for both their health and their wealth. Too often the Right concentrates on cerebral issues – like debt and deficits – that appeal to senses located above our necks (and involve concepts that only policy wonks could love). And we lose. We lose because in politics, it is the emotions that exist between the neck and the knees that usually determine outcomes, emotions that are usually centred round the location of people's wallets.

The real key and primary political advantage of opt-out health savings accounts is that they offer a way out of the entitlement mentality trap by offering voters something better – far better – than getting their taxes back through Medicare. The benefits would not simply flow to government budgets; the real winners would be those who opt-out and reap the financial benefits from choosing a more efficient and cost-effective way to insure their health in the form of higher health savings account balances and ultimately higher retirement incomes. Political support for opting out of Medicare could be mobilised by selling the 'hip pocket' advantages to individuals, and could be sold as both a tax cut and a real increase in lifetime incomes.

The only way for the Right to achieve significant health reform is to build a constituency that supports change within the community with sufficient political punch to overcome the vested interests embedded in the current health system that are opposed to doing things differently. I believe there is a natural constituency on the Right and throughout middle Australia waiting to be tapped, which will support opt-out health saving accounts when given the choice to opt-in to a financially beneficial private alternative to Medicare.

Getting Back to Basics: Law-Making 101

Lorraine Finlay

Lorraine Finlay is a lecturer in the School of Law at Murdoch University

*The ten most dangerous words in the English language are
"Hi, I'm from the government, and I'm here to help".'*

(Ronald Reagan, 28 July 1988)

Ever since the then-Leader of the Opposition walked onto the stage at the ALP national conference in 2007 and announced "My name is Kevin, I'm from Queensland and I'm here to help" the Australian Government has been helping us all at a feverish pace. If we are being honest, the trend started well before Kevin '07. But it has certainly picked up speed over the past decade. The level of activity has been exhausting but, despite (mostly) the best of government intentions, it is doubtful whether most Australians have been left feeling any better off.

Modern politics seems to be ruled by the need for constant activity. Too often it is activity for the sake of activity. If there is a problem, then you need to be seen to be doing something. Anything! There is very little room for reflection or reference to longer-term results. In terms of law-making, this is enormously problematic. We seem to have forgotten that laws and government are not the ends in themselves. Rather, they are supposed to be a means to an end – specifically life, liberty and security for each individual citizen.

This chapter will put forward an argument that is rarely heard in the current, hyper-frenetic Australian political environment, namely that we should put the brakes on government. Government is not the answer to every question. Or, indeed, to most questions. In fact, we need less government, not more. Our aim should be fewer laws, not more.

When we look at each of the different branches and levels of government in Australia we can see how far many of our national institutions have crept beyond their original remit. The first task of law reform in Australia should be to remind the very institutions we have entrusted with making, administering and interpreting our laws of their original briefs. This includes the legislative, executive and judicial branches of government, as well as the national government in terms of our current federal system. Each of these has grown well beyond expectations, with significant consequences for Australian democracy.

Laws, laws everywhere!

It seems there isn't a problem these days to which the answer isn't the introduction of a new law! Certainly, the measure of a successful government and parliament seems to be just how many laws they are able to introduce during their term in office. At least, this has appeared to be the key measure in recent years, with Ministers frequently emphasizing the success of the 43rd Parliament (in particular) by reference to how many pieces of legislation had been passed.[1] Indeed, the 543 Acts of Parliament that were passed during Julia Gillard's tenure as Prime Minister were apparently enough to qualify her as Australia's most productive Prime Minister![2] By this measure, our first national Parliaments were terrible failures. It took over eight years for our first Australian parliamentarians to pass enough laws to match the 206 Acts that our national politicians were able to pass in 2015 alone.[3] It wasn't that our first parliamentarians were lazy. Rather, our current Parliaments are over-zealous law-makers who see creating more laws as being a key part of their job description.

Of course, any sensible person knows that the sheer quantity of legislation passed is no guarantee of either quality or success. All that it does guarantee is that government is intruding more than ever into all of our lives. For anybody who believes in reducing the role of government and maximizing the freedom of the individual this should be of concern. When our default position to any difficult issue is to demand that the government should do something about it – and preferably introduce new laws to deal with the problem – then we know that a serious conversation in Australia about the role of government is well overdue. Good governance is about much more than law-making.

Recapturing the sovereignty of Parliament

When Robert Menzies considered *The Task of Democracy* during *The Forgotten People* broadcasts in 1942 he spoke of two things that democracy must do "if it is to be a real force in the new world". The first was to "recapture the vision of the good of man as the purpose

---

[1] See, for example, Peter van Onselen, "Volume of legislation doesn't stack up for Labor", *The Australian*, 22 June 2013.

[2] Nick Evershed, "Was Julia Gillard the most productive prime minister in Australia's history?", *The Guardian* 28 June 2013.

[3] Australian Government, *Alphabetical Table of Acts*.

of government" and the second was to "restore the authority and prestige of Parliament as the supreme organic expression of self-government".[4] Today this task seems more daunting than ever before, with the authority and prestige of Parliament seemingly at an all-time low.

Undoubtedly one consequence of the slim majority or even minority governments that have been the norm in recent years is the temptation for governments to bypass the Parliament and to instead govern through the Executive arm as much as possible. This has only further strengthened the dominance of the Executive over the Parliament in Australia, a feature of the Australian political landscape that has now become firmly entrenched at the national level.

While Australia's fused political system has always accepted a closer entwining of the Executive and Legislative branches of government than a strict separation of powers would otherwise tolerate, there must be limits to this. The most important is that the Legislature cannot abdicate its legislative responsibilities and must ensure that parliamentary oversight of the Executive is retained.

The sheer size of Executive Government in Australia today makes effective parliamentary oversight all but impossible. While the explosive growth in the overall volume of legislation is noted above, this is nothing compared to the exponential growth of Executive Government and the Australian Public Service. It is no exaggeration to say that Australia has evolved into a bureaucratic democracy! At the Commonwealth level, we are currently administered by 42 Ministers & Assistant Ministers (administering 53 portfolios), 18 government departments, 192 individual government agencies[5] and, as at 30

---

[4] Robert Menzies, "Chapter 36 – The Task of Democracy", *The Forgotten People*, 13 November 1942.
[5] See Australian Government, *List of Departments and Agencies*.

June 2015, 152,430 Australian public servants.[6] A quick search of the federal register of legislation lists 2139 legislative instruments as being made in 2015, and an astonishing 61,450 legislative instruments as being made during the past ten years. By contrast, the Parliament itself passed fewer Acts in the past ten years in total (specifically 1,821) than there were legislative instruments made in 2015 alone. The primary law-making institution in Australia is no longer the Australian Parliament, but rather the Executive and, specifically, the Australian Public Service.

Restoring the primacy of Parliament as the key law-making institution and the central driver of policy debate in Australia is an important element in revitalizing democracy in Australia and re-connecting our people to our politics. Is it any wonder that so many Australians feel disconnected from politics when so many key decisions seem to be getting made by bureaucrats in Canberra who are unelected and unaccountable? The observations of Menzies ring true over seventy years later:[7]

> The sovereignty of Parliament. That is a great phrase and a vital truth. If only we could all understand it to the full, what a change we would make! Sovereignty is the quality of kingship, and democracy brings it to the poor man's door.

Quasi-Judicial Activists

In a similar vein, when unelected and unaccountable judges step beyond their judicial role and enter the political realm our democracy is weakened. The judicial role is a critical one in a country such as Australia where the rule of law is central. When judges start to veer

---

[6] Australian Public Service Commission, *APS Statistical Bulletin 2014-15* (14 September 2015).
[7] Robert Menzies, "Chapter 36 – The Task of Democracy", *The Forgotten People*, 13 November 1942.

from the judicial towards the political, the rule of law is necessarily undermined.

Over the past decade the High Court of Australia has certainly been less adventurous than the activist high watermark of the Mason High Court which, at times, seemed to be using a special "invisible ink" version of the Australian Constitution that allowed them to discover all sorts of constitutional extras that nobody else had known were there. Still, there have been enough examples of judicial activism in recent years – the discovery of implied constitutional voting rights in *Roach v Electoral Commissioner*[8] and *Rowe v Electoral Commissioner*[9] being an obvious example – to remind us just how important it is to appoint judges in Australia that have a clear understanding of the judicial role and its necessary limits.

Even more concerning in recent years, however, has been the growing activist trend amongst quasi-judicial bodies in Australia. The most obvious example of this has been the Australian Human Rights Commission ("AHRC"). While the AHRC is not a judicial body, it has appeared to try and deflect criticism by highlighting its independent status.[10] The AHRC certainly does have important functions of inquiry, dispute resolution and advocacy, and it is important that its independence is maintained and respected. However, it is dangerous to suggest that any institution in a democratic nation should be beyond reproach or immune from criticism.

The AHRC is no different to any other government body in this respect. Examples such as the delaying of the public inquiry into children in detention because of seemingly political considerations, the complete lack of regard for due process in the treatment of three QUT students against whom a s. 18C complaint was lodged

[8] (2007) 233 CLR 162.
[9] (2010) 243 CLR 1.
[10] See, for example, George Brandis, "Human Rights Commission and Gillian Triggs not above reproach", *The Australian*, 27 February 2015.

in the AHRC, and the recent example of the Race Discrimination Commission ignoring any semblance of objectivity by publicly encouraging s. 18C complaints following the publication of the controversial Bill Leak cartoon,[11] highlight the partisan and activist path that the AHRC has trodden in recent times. The AHRC will no doubt argue that it has to be free to criticize human rights violations wherever and whenever they occur in Australia, and that part of its job is to hold the government to account. This is undoubtedly true. However, in doing so it shouldn't expect that it will be immune from criticism – particularly when its actions move it beyond a role of independent oversight to full engagement in partisan activism.

The role between the judicial function and political activism should not be blurred. If a judge (or a Human Rights Commissioner for that matter) wants to become involved in partisan politics they are as free as any other citizen to do so, provided that they resign their commission, stride openly into the political arena, and accept that they are not immune from criticism when they engage in political debate.

The Ever-Expanding Reach of the Commonwealth

Compounding the problems described above is the fact that it generally isn't just one government trying to introduce new laws to show that they are doing something about the latest *cause célèbre*. All too frequently in Australia we find multiple governments – State and Federal – all trying to do something about the same issue at the same time. This was not what was intended at the time of Federation. The Founding Fathers intended for the Australian Constitution to provide the national parliament with a list of enumerated and limited

---

[11] Chris Merritt, "Race Commissioner has blatantly prejudged Bill Leak over cartoon", *The Australian*, 12 August 2016.

subjects of national importance over which it was to have power, with all other issues being left to the individual States.

This has not been how the Australian political landscape has developed in practice. Instead, the political power of the Commonwealth has proved to be ever-expanding – helped by a variety of factors, including its fiscal dominance over the States and a Commonwealth-friendly High Court of Australia. The extent of Commonwealth expansion can be readily seen by looking at the recent 2016 election campaign. Both major parties made significant promises in areas that lay well beyond what have traditionally been accepted as areas of Commonwealth responsibility. For example, the ALP promised over $40 million to make sure that every Australian child had swimming lessons[12] while the Coalition promised to invest an additional $60 million to extend the *Sporting Schools Programme* to help increase children's participation in sport.[13] There is no doubt that encouraging children to participate in sport is highly desirable. But it is difficult to argue that it falls into the same category as defence, immigration or foreign relations as a policy area that necessarily requires the intervention of a national government.

Further, entrance by the Commonwealth Government into a particular policy area is not necessarily (or ordinarily) accompanied by a neatly corresponding State Government exit. More often than not, what we are left with is duplication, confusion and blame-shifting between the State and Federal levels. This duplication is frequently pointed to by critics of federalism as a problem inherent in the concept, and a reason that State Governments should be swept aside as an antiquated reflection of our colonial past.[14] However, as Greg

---

[12] Australian Labor Party, *Water Safe: Labor's Plan to Help our Kids Swim and Survive* (Media Release, 15 May 2016).

[13] Liberal Party of Australia, *The Coalition's Policy for More Sport in Our Schools* (2016 Federal Election).

[14] See, for example, Lindsay Tanner, "Abolish the States", *New Matilda*, 22 November 2005.

Craven has astutely observed:[15]

> ... much of the difficulty in this context has occurred because the Commonwealth, through use of its financial muscle, has invaded State areas, such as education and health. Confusion of accountability and responsibility thus may be sheeted home to Commonwealth incursion, not State incompetence. In these circumstances, a reasonable State response might well be that if the Commonwealth is prepared to vacate the field and leave the cheque behind, the State would be more than happy to eliminate all elements of division and overlap.

Reform of our Federation remains one of the great missed opportunities of the Abbott years. The promised White Paper into the Reform of the Federation has been consigned to the scrapheap and the prospects for substantial reform are looking grim. The closest we have come to a federalism reform agenda under the Turnbull Government was the pre-COAG Prime Ministerial "thought bubble" that perhaps the States should be allowed to raise or share in income taxes. In itself, this is an idea worthy of further exploration. However, modernizing Commonwealth-State fiscal arrangements is a substantive policy area that needs a well-planned, longer-term roadmap to reform and certainly can't be achieved through a single doorstop media interview.

Where to From Here?

There has truly never been a more exciting time in Australia to be a law-maker! As a nation we are making more laws than ever before and, whether you are part of the federal Executive, Legislature or Judiciary, each branch of government is (to various degrees) venturing into new

---

[15] Greg Craven, 'The New Centralism and the Collapse of the Conservative Constitution' (Paper presented at the Department of the Senate Occasional Lecture Series, Parliament House, Canberra, 2005), 138.

and uncharted territories. Of course, this is overwhelmingly to the detriment of both the Australian people and Australian democracy.

The answer is far from simple. But a good starting point would be to go back to basics. A kind of Law-Making 101. It is worth reminding ourselves of what these institutions were originally created to do, and why they were originally limited in the way that they were. In all of the chaos and excitement of Australian politics in recent years, values have been far too easily swept aside. We need to return to our basic political values and ask some key questions about our governance and legal frameworks. Simply creating lots of laws and doing more things does not mean you are a good government.

Religion and the New Sectarianism:

Countering the Call for Silence

Peter Kurti

Research Fellow, Religion and Civil Society,
Centre for Independent Studies

Faith and the Call to Silence

Religion is being pushed forcefully to the margins of public debate in Australia and the values of religious citizens discounted as either meaningless or irrelevant when it comes to the consideration of key social issues. Behind the apparent inclusiveness of our open, secular society lurks a spectre of intolerance which calls for the silencing of dissenting voices, especially when those voices are religious. This is the 'new sectarianism' where religion – especially Christianity – is deemed unworthy and unacceptable. One of the principal tasks for the conservative side of politics – or the political Right, notable for its commitment to the autonomy and the dignity of the individual human person, is to counter this call for silence and to ensure that all citizens – both the religious and those of no faith – can participate fully and effectively in Australian democratic society.

The latest push against religion is coming from those who want to legalise euthanasia – or 'physician-assisted suicide' as it's commonly called. According to assisted dying advocate TV producer Andrew Denton, religion has no part whatsoever to play in this – or any other – debate, especially when it comes to moral questions about the meaning and value of human life. In a widely reported speech to the National Press Club calling for the introduction of assisted dying laws in Australia, Denton said that religious people need to butt out of the debate and not impose their views on anyone else. "I urge you, step aside," Denton said, directing his remarks to those "whose beliefs instruct you that only God can decide how a human being should die."[1] If you've got religion, in other words, sit down, shut up, and don't be a pest.

When it comes to making medical decisions about who can die and when, the new sectarians apparently already know everything there is to know about human suffering. Those who agree with them are welcome to speak up; but any with opposing views must remain silent. Denton, however, went on in his address to level a more sinister charge. Frustrated that his own views have not yet carried the day in the federal Parliament, he accused politicians who oppose him for faith-based reasons of comprising a "theocracy hidden inside our democracy." It is a fantastic nonsense. Religious politicians aren't hidden away in some secret congress; their views, openly expressed, may simply be more influential than Denton wants. And since a theocracy is a government run by clerics ruling in the name of a god or gods, Denton's remarks are actually an insult to every democratically elected politician who happens to have an active religious faith.

Assisted dying is not the only contentious social issue where the new sectarians think they know what's best for us. The story is the same when it comes to same-sex marriage, gender diversity, and exploring sexuality in the classroom. Anyone who believes in a God, or gods, must pack up and vacate the public square. Religion is dismissed as

---

[1] Andrew Denton, National Press Club, 10 August 2016

having nothing useful to say about any of these contentious topics; and anyone who questions this hard line sectarian orthodoxy is condemned as a hateful, fanatical bigot.

The move on the part of the sectarian *bien pensants* to exclude religion from public conversations is only the latest in the relentless drift towards an illiberal intolerance of the views of the faithful. Opponents of religion defend their assault by insisting that God – seen variously as too timid, too militant, or completely redundant – is on the way out, so religion can hardly be said to count any longer. When it comes to Christianity in Australia, recent research indicates that the number of people identifying as Christians declined over two years by 8.3% – from 60.9% in 2011 to 52.6% in 2013 – while the number of those declaring no religious affiliation rose from 29.2% to 37.6% in the same period.[2] Whereas Christianity appears to be losing ground, however, other religions are gaining prominence. The 2011 Census recorded that a little over 2% of Australians identified as Muslim and about 2.5% identify as Buddhists. Both numbers are expected to increase, although by 2050 it is estimated that Muslims will comprise just 4.9%. Even though the statistics indicate an apparent decline in religious observance, the numbers show there is still a significant proportion of Australians who express some form of religious belief. Their values, cultures and customs are, in turn, shaped by those beliefs. Yet it appears that Denton and his smart set are intent only upon shutting down Christians – especially Catholics – and excluding them from public discussion. They are unlikely any time soon to accuse, say, Australian Muslims of forming a hidden theocracy and urge them to step aside from public debate.

---

[2] 'Christians in Australia nearing minority status as religious affiliation declines sharply since 2011', *Roy Morgan Research*, (16 April 2014)

Religion and the Roots of the Individual

Concerns were expressed in some quarters that the Australian Bureau of Statistics' decision to move the option of 'No Religion' to the top of the list for the 2016 census could lead to a very marked shift away from the nation's vestigial Christian identity.[3] It has become almost commonplace to hold that this kind of shift is a symptom of the grip that secularisation has on western nations such as Australia, forcing religion out of what is widely referred to as the 'public sphere'. The fervour of anti-religious sectarians is fuelled by their conviction that we are witnesses to the decline and decay of institutional religion. It may be a widely held view, but is it accurate?

'Religion' is a term with a very elastic definition. One way of understanding it is as any system of belief in a supreme being that encourages and sustains practices, values and experiences of a certain kind that, while possibly grounded in historical occurrence, are described in the language of myth and metaphor. "Religious stories are to civilizations what dreams are to individuals," says David Tacey. "They are symbolically encoded messages from the depths of the human soul."[4] The truth of religious claims, therefore, does not reside in the results of an empirical test for meaning; it resides in the cultural imagination of the socially connected individual. Even though some forms of religious life appear to be growing in Australia, these social connections are changing.

The overall decline of religion as a social and cultural force is frequently associated with the decline of other traditional social institutions. Where formerly religion more effectively reinforced ties of family, community and nation, today those ties are weakening, along with the religious sentiments that used to underpin them,

[3] Charis Chang, 'Unholy war over census question on religion', *News.com.au* (5 August 2016)
[4] David Tacey, *Beyond Literal Belief: Religion as Metaphor*, (Mulgrave VIC: Garratt Publishing, 2015), 1, 5

at mounting and under-appreciated cost. For instance, the loss of traditional family and community ties – which used to motivate citizens to undertake voluntary work in the various fields of social welfare – is in turn putting increased economic and political pressure on governments that are forced to step into the breach and fund an array of substitute care and support services for vulnerable groups of both young and old citizens.[5]

Weakened though it may be in some western liberal democracies, religion is not yet dead, however. The end of religion in those societies, promised by "assorted western intellectuals" for nearly 300 years according to Rodney Stark, is one of the consequences of secularisation.[6] This refers, broadly, to the cultural displacement of religion by other social systems of organisation and meaning, and the consequent loss of religion's authority in society. Nowadays, however, scholars – including, most notably, Peter Berger who has been an ardent proponent of the secularisation thesis – are raising more widely questions about the accuracy of the secularisation thesis.[7] It is becoming ever more important to be sceptical of the secular, liberal idea that religion is simply dying out. In this fluid environment in which what were formerly held to be the eternal verities are anything but, it is also becoming more important to understand the complex relationship between religion and the democratic liberties we enjoy in this country. Indeed, defenders of religion in the public sphere are making more frequent appeals to the religious – and more usually, Christian – roots of western civilisation.

---

[5] See for example Mary Eberstadt, *How The West Really Lost God: A New Theory of Secularization*, (Conshohocken PA: Templeton Press, 2013) [Kindle edition]

[6] Rodney Stark, 'Secularization, R.I.P', *Sociology of Religion*, Vol.60 No.3 (autumn 1999), 249-273

[7] See, for example, Peter Berger, 'The Good of Religious Pluralism' *First Things* (April 2016), 39-42, and David Martin, 'Has Secularization gone into Reverse?' in David Martin, *The Future of Christianity: Reflections on Violence and Democracy, Religion and Secularization*, (Farnham, UK: Ashgate, 2011).

Intellectual historians such as Larry Siedentop have developed compelling arguments that Christianity, with its central egalitarian moral insight about individual liberty, played a decisive part in the development of the individual and the concept of individual liberty. The emergence of the free, sovereign individual brought with it a new social status that expressed individual agency and the capacity to give informed consent, together with a legally enforceable right to exercise liberty.[8]

Sovereignty of the individual is one of the cardinal tenets of classical liberal thought. It is a freedom grounded in reason. This sovereignty of the autonomous individual entails that he or she takes priority over the family, tribe or community while remaining informed by the values, cultures, beliefs and customs of the clan. Indeed, it is the very fabric of community life that forms the social context within which the individual develops the capacity for reason in which freedom is grounded. Religion is a crucial component of what political scientist Joshua Mitchell describes as this "mysterious and ineffable" social fabric. It's mysterious and ineffable, he says, because when absent, it cannot be manufactured at will:

> The hallowed institutions that make such education unto reason and freedom possible are the family, churches and synagogues, local schools, a free press, and civic associations – all of which form citizens-in-training so that they become fit for self-governance.[9]

---

[8] For a more detailed examination of Siedentop's argument, see Peter Kurti, 'Secular Prejudice and the Survival of Religious Freedom', *Quadrant*, (November 2014, Vol LVIII, No. II), 36-40

[9] Joshua Mitchell, 'The Age of Exhaustion', *The American Interest*, (Vol.11 No.2 2015)

Religion, the Citizen, and the Public Sphere

Australian society has deep roots in religious principles and values. Indeed, one of the basic issues facing Australian society during the course of the nation's history has not been that of securing the removal of religion from public life but rather that of managing religious pluralism. According to Greg Melleuish and Stephen Chavura, who have evaluated the influence of religion in Australia and argued against the myth of Australia as a uniquely secular country, "A primary concern was to ensure that religious difference did not turn into religious conflict, thereby creating a social order riven by violent…activities."[10] Melleuish and Chavura dismiss the idea that Australia is somehow uniquely secular as an "illusion, brought on by an inadequate understanding of what religion, and the religious condition, mean, together with a dash of wishful thinking."[11]

But whereas religion was – and in many respects, continues to be – an important element of Australian society, our country has never been an autocratic theocracy (such as Iran) where politics serves religion. We are, thankfully, a parliamentary democracy where religion can serve and inform politics without ever assuming precedence over it. Arguments for the importance of religion to our conception of freedom are, themselves, grounded in empirical claims about the significance of religious belief and practice for the wellbeing of our society. A commitment to a free and open society demands that we never underestimate the importance of religion to the health, liberty and prosperity of that society. As Marcus Smith and Peter Harden have argued with particular reference to Christianity:

> Aside from the fruitlessness of efforts to preclude religion from
> public life, the ideal of democracy is best served by a vibrant

---

[10] Greg Melleuish and Stephen Chavura, 'Utilitarianism contra Sectarianism' in William Coleman (ed.), *Only in Australia: The History, Politics, and Economics of Australian Exceptionalism* (Oxford, UK: OUP, 2016), 65

[11] Greg Melleuish and Stephen Chavura, as above, 63

plurality that reflects the diversity of the human condition and the virtue of equality that has strong roots in the Christian tradition. In a more pragmatic sense, overlap of the religious and secular perhaps offers the best safeguard to irrationalities of both traditions that tend to occur when either is adhered to in isolation.[12]

Once the centrality of religion to the social fabric is acknowledged, one of the key challenges for the political Right becomes the need to secure the place of religion in what is sometimes referred as the "public sphere". According to comparative religion scholar Gavin Flood, the notion of the public sphere emerged in the course of the 17th and 18th centuries and is to be understood as "the shared arena where subjectivities can be displayed and where the institutions that an individual invests in can find articulation."[13] Far from being a neutral space, this shared arena is often contested. As Flood notes, the public sphere is:

> A place of discourse and is integral to the governments we have and the laws we abide by... It is the realm wherein debate can take place not only about legislation and governance but about the deeper values that inform them, about what it is to lead a good life and what justice is.[14]

If the public sphere is understood as the arena where members of society can come to a common mind about matters of common interest, it is reasonable to hold that religion must have a place in that sphere. After all, religions already coexist in civil society, participating in the discourse of contemporary political life and contributing to discussion about the shape of politics needed to

---

[12] Marcus Smith and Peter Marden, 'Capturing the Religious Spirit: A Challenge for the Secular State', *Journal of Church and State* Vol.55, No. 1 (2012), 23-49, 35
[13] Gavin Flood, *The Importance of Religion: Meaning and Action in Our Strange World* (Chichester, UK: Wiley-Blackwell, 2012), 191
[14] Gavin Flood, as above, 192

foster the development of the good life. But as Flood notes, it is in this discourse that "difference and conflict occur between religions, and between religions and the secular state". Religions are often critical of the secular state, wanting it to do less of some things and more of others, and criticising it for moral shortcomings in policies ranging from border protection to social security to climate change to freedom of speech. In expressing those views, religious believers seek to participate fully as secular citizens whilst upholding the principles of their faith traditions. Hence, as Flood observes, "most religious people today negotiate multiple identities as religious persons, as holders of jobs, as parents, as children, as politicians".[15]

This negotiation of multiple identities can generate problems for the liberal state that needs to strike a balance between the claims of the religious citizen and those of the state. A good example of one problem is the French response of *laïcité* – an official state policy intended to restrict, and possibly eliminate, religious influence over the state. *Laïcité* imposes a tolerance boundary beyond which religion must not intrude. But this demand for conformity to state policy, whilst presented as one that is politically neutral, is actually quite illiberal in many respects because of its restrictive concept of citizenship. Thus, citizens of the French secular state are limited in how they give public expression to their religious beliefs by, for example, wearing the *hijab* or displaying a crucifix. It can seem an attractive approach for those who wish to see religion relegated entirely from the public sphere to the private. But such demands for strict conformity can bring the religious citizen into conflict with the state.

A different form of conflict in the negotiation of multiple identities can arise when a secular state, such as Australia, allows the religious citizen free expression of his or her beliefs, but that expression

---

[15] Gavin Flood, as above, 194

potentially involves some hostility towards either the laws of the state or, in some cases, the very existence of the state. Demands, for example, by some Muslim communities for the recognition of the superiority of sharia law over secular law represent a challenge to the sovereignty of the secular state. Similarly, the call for the recognition of cultural practices such as female genital mutilation or child marriage generate conflict with the wider community not simply because they are considered incompatible with Australian secular social norms, but because they flatly contravene Australian secular law.

In responding to this kind of conflict, the new sectarians are right to insist that the claims and norms of the wider, secular community must take precedence over those of a religious tradition. But when the conflict is softer – in that it does not pose a threat to the legal or political integrity of the state – a more nuanced response is called for. The challenge for those on the Right of politics is to articulate a more subtle account of the relationship between the religious citizen and the secular state. One approach is to recall the claims of citizenship – both in terms of benefits and obligations – that the state makes of all its citizens. As Flood notes, "Democracy entails citizenship and the legitimacy of democracy arises from the supposition that it is a form of governance that promotes the equal interests of all its members."[16]

Sectarian critics seeking to deny religion a voice in the public sphere invariably overlook the Australian Constitution when pressing their case, yet the Constitution does imply some religious features of citizenship. It does this by making a form of provision for the freedom of religious citizens to give expression to their beliefs – not in the sense of granting a constitutional *right* to the free expression of religion, nor by conferring a right to assert freedom

---

[16] Gavin Flood, as above, 202

of religion against the actions of other individuals or organisations. Rather, the Constitution does so by placing a limit on the legislative power of the federal Parliament. The Constitution thereby secures religious freedom for the citizen by constraint rather than the creation of an enforceable right.[17] Even so, as Wayne Hudson has argued, there are significant components here of a definition of religious citizenship that combines two elements: first, that of a 'civil society' understanding – whereby religious citizenship is that which religious citizens exercise in the civic sphere; second, that of a 'rights of the person' understanding – whereby citizens are allowed to exercise religious freedoms but must also extend that right to others, tolerating differences in the ways that citizens enact their social life.[18]

Countering the 'New Sectarian' Threat to the Religious Citizen

The new sectarians aim, at best to override, and, at worst, to obliterate the preferences and values of religious citizens by arguing that the interests of the wider, secular community must always outweigh those of the individual. Yet the flourishing of the individual citizen must always be a central concern of liberal democracy – especially in a conservative account of democracy. Human flourishing, of course, is seldom a solitary affair and will occur within the lived context of community where the individual's identity is always bound up

---

[17] Section 116 of the Australian Constitution states: 'The Commonwealth shall not make any law for establishing any religion, or for imposing any religious observance, or for prohibiting the free exercise of any religion, and no religious test shall be required as a qualification for any office or public trust under the Commonwealth.' See also Carolyn Evans, *Legal Protection of Religious Freedom in Australia* (Leichhardt, NSW: Federation Press, 2012), 72, and Peter Kurti, *The Forgotten Freedom: Threats to Religious Liberty in Australia* (St Leonards NSW: The Centre for Independent Studies, 2014).

[18] Wayne Hudson, 'Religious Citizenship', *Australian Journal of Politics and History*, vol. 59, no 3, (September 2003)

with communal narratives of tradition. This is particularly so in the case of the religious citizen who is immersed in the narratives and traditions of a faith community. Flood has remarked elegantly: "As [religious] citizens we abide by the law but pursue our enlightenment or salvation in the communities to which we belong and from which we draw the sap of our life."[19]

Questions about what it is to lead a good life, what justice is – and what kind of society we wish to have – concern every Australian. In a free and open society, where everyone is entitled to debate and discuss these matters of common interest, religious citizens will have their own views about these issues and are as entitled as any other citizen to express them. The health of our society depends on permitting those citizens to debate not only the laws that govern us but also the deeper values that inform those laws. Freedom to strike an appropriate balance between the claims of modernity and tradition must be upheld for all. Opponents of religion frequently base their opposition on a conviction that the explanatory capacities of science and technology render religious belief redundant. But as critics such as Terry Eagleton have argued, religion does not compete with science to offer explanations of reality. Rather it offers a vision of how human beings are to live together, identifying love as the ideal focal point of human history. Eagleton has given an insightful account of what faith – specifically Christian faith – means to him, and it is worth quoting in full:

> Faith...is not primarily a belief that something or someone exists, but a commitment and allegiance — faith *in* something which might make a difference to the frightful situation you find yourself in, as is the case, say, with faith in feminism or anti-colonialism. It is not in the first place a question of signing up to a description of reality, though it certainly involves that as well. Christian faith,

---

19 Gavin Flood, as above, 205

as I understand it, is not primarily a matter of signing on for the proposition that there exists a Supreme Being, but the kind of commitment made manifest by a human at the end of his tether, foundering in darkness, pain, and bewilderment, who nevertheless remains faithful to the promise of transformative love.[20]

Dissident, religious voices are being raised in public debates about contentious social issues that go to the heart of our life together, such as: who should be able to get married; what children should be taught in our schools; and whether human life is ours to take or ours to nurture. These voices are an important component of Australian civil society because they challenge the prevailing opinions of the day and give expression to the views of citizens whose participation in the life of the secular state is informed by a matrix of traditions, values and cultural norms that do not always sit easily alongside those of modernity. Yet democracy promotes the interests of all citizens, regardless of their beliefs, allowing them to uphold and express their beliefs but binding them to act within the law as they do so. Given the importance both of religion to the Australian social fabric and of the benefits and obligations of citizenship, why should the new sectarians expect to be able to banish religion from public discourse?

The political Right must be alert to the threat posed by the new sectarianism that is part of a general move to silence dissident religious voices that speak out in public. For one thing, this silencing is a move that represents an encroaching intolerance; for another, it represents a threat to Australian social and cultural bastions to which political conservatives have been traditionally committed. Australians who incline towards the centre-Right are characterised, in the broadest terms, by an innate social, cultural and political

---

[20] Terry Eagleton, Reason, *Faith and Revolution: Reflections on the God Debate*, (New Haven: Yale University Press, 2009), 37

conservatism which includes sympathy for many of the values affirmed by religion. A betrayal of these values by the political Right could ultimately prove to be a betrayal of much of Middle Australia – with predictably dire electoral consequences for culpable political parties. The Right must act now to recall the foundational principles of our democracy, call out the new sectarianism, and counter the call to silence.

Interest Rate Policy

Steven Kates

Associate Professor of Economics at RMIT

There are few if any aspects of the economy more potentially dangerous and destabilising than the area of money and credit creation. Mismanagement of the financial side of an economy will keep economic growth to a minimum and leave large parts of the community with a far lower standard of living than they might otherwise have had. The instability caused by financial panics and crises are legendary, and remain a problem to this day. The political advantages of low rates of interest and the fostering of the pretence of growth, ensure that government interference over interest rate policy is almost guaranteed to drive an economy in the wrong direction. The more recent invention of a separate and independent agency in charge of interest rate adjustment, where governments remain at arm's length from policy decisions, is to some extent an improvement, although governments can never really be kept away from the decision making process in such an important area of policy. What is therefore necessary is that the policy settings of these semi-independent money-creation interest-rate-setting agencies are based on a sound theoretical foundation. That, unfortunately, we do not have. But that is the essence of what is required if monetary and credit policies are to provide the foundation for strong growth and higher real incomes.

The core question in discussing monetary policy and credit creation is who gets to use the nation's savings. But that in turn raises the question what those savings consist of. Because the great problem in discussing monetary policy in the modern age is that for almost everyone, savings are conceived of in terms of money, when savings, so far as economic growth is concerned, actually consist of real resources that can be used in productive activity.

If someone wants to build a factory they need labour, bricks and mortar. But to get the various inputs, they first need money or at least a line of credit. The modern approach to looking at such things is to begin and end with the question: where will the *money* come from? The proper approach is to think about where will the *resources* come from, and most importantly, what those resources could have been used to produce instead.

Our savings, properly understood, consist of the resources available with which to build our productive investments. They are always in short supply. Even in the midst of recessions, such resources remain scarce. They are never free goods. In the midst of recession, a larger proportion of such resources are unemployed. This is because, in a recession, some of businesses find that they can no longer sell what they produce at prices high enough to cover their costs. A recession is thus a period in which resources are re-deployed away from their current uses and find their way elsewhere, just as the employees of such enterprises must do. A loss-making enterprise drags an economy down, and however difficult it may be for the owners and their employees, this is what an adjustment process requires.

Moreover, some of the capital that had been previously used in such enterprises will have become completely redundant, and cannot be used in any profitable enterprise anywhere else in the economy. The housing stock in some remote region becomes literally valueless if the mine that made the town economically viable stops producing. An input is valuable only to the extent that the output it is a component of covers its full production costs.

There is thus a continual need to renew our capital stock and it is only the availability of productive resources that allows this to happen. It is these productive resources that constitute our savings, which is where the credit creation process comes in.

What interest rates do is determine who will get their hands on these scarce savings. What is borrowed is, of course, money. What is sought is, of course, a proportion of the nation's available productive resources. To mistake money for the resources required is a major conceptual error but one made at every turn.

There is, nevertheless, no doubt that to get their hands on the resources someone must first borrow the money. What interest rates once upon a time did was rise to the point where the amounts supplied and demanded for these resources were equal. The competition for resources kept rates up, since it was the real demand for inputs that made the difference. Money rates of interest more or less mirrored the real side of the economy.

But the existence of money and the credit creation process have always been the weak links in the process. Financial mania is an old story that you can read about going back to the days of the Roman Empire. Get-rich schemes have always attracted those who see an opportunity to make their fortune by borrowing funds for some project or another. The frequency that borrowers have pulled down those who had lent to them as well is one of the constant tales of enterprise, and pre-dates the arrival of the capitalist system. The misdirected use of savings continues to this very day, and cannot be avoided.

The other side of this same equation is the appropriation of our savings by governments. Governments have always had their own purposes, whether to wage war or merely enrich themselves or their friends. If they could not tax enough, there were various means to subvert the currency. Coin clipping is an antique technique employed across the millennia. Today, with every currency a national currency, and fiat paper money the medium of exchange, the ability for governments to put their hands on a nation's savings by printing more money has never been greater. With the arrival of Keynesian economics, which not just permits a government to deplete a nation's savings, but actively encourages it to do so, since it is even argued that such spending, irrespective of what such spending is on, is good for future economic growth, our national savings have never been at greater risk.

What then to do?

How, then, should interest rate policy be managed. Here is a five point program. Yet in putting these points forward in the abstract, there is always the need to play some facets of economic policy by ear since there are so many different configurations an economy can take. Nevertheless, monetary policy within a market economy has to be conducted with the recognition that virtually all of the adjustment that takes place must be based on the activities of individuals who are confronting their own sets of circumstances and are in need of market signals that will relay to them accurate information about the nature of the economy they are operating in. Obscuring these signals, or even worse, causing these signals to misrepresent the underlying reality, is what interest rate policy must not, as an absolute first priority, do. Easier said than done, but unless market participants – that is, entrepreneurs, employees, the owners of capital, savers and lenders – have a reasonably sound understanding of what is going on, an economy will not perform as well as it might.

First, we have to understand that the primary purpose of interest rates is to allocate national savings to their most productive uses, which in turn means we have to understand that our savings are made up of real resources, which are in very limited supply. Of money, there is always plenty, and if we want more, there is never much trouble in conjuring up an additional supply. The financial system, starting from our central banks and working outwards, can produce money almost at will.

We have been accustomed to thinking of savings as an amount of money without an immediate and direct association with the limited supply of resources that are available for use in adding to our stock of capital assets. Investment means building productive assets that are intended to increase our future ability to produce. There will always be money in the bank. The frequent reference to these supposedly unspent savings is merely a form of economic illiteracy.

Our actual savings consist of the resources that are being used to extend our productive capabilities. Of these, every economy is in short supply. While it is easy to point to money held in banks, it is much less easy to point to assets that are not only resting idle but where their owners are not doing what they can to find somewhere these assets can be used where they can receive a positive return.

Capital assets often become unemployed. A factory may close but the building it sits in remains, as does the machinery that was used as part of the production process. The owner of the building will try to find someone else to rent or buy the premises. The machinery will be sold to those who can use these assets, and if no buyer can be found, may be sold for scrap. Indeed, some of the machinery may not even have scrap value and be taken to the tip and thrown away. In real terms there are seldom if ever savings that are not put to use if a use can be found. Markets are hugely efficient in this way.

The probability that productive assets will not find their way to a profitable use if such uses exist is small.

Second, we have to stop using interest rates as an anti-inflation policy tool. The Great Inflation of the 1970s and 80s was eventually subdued through increases in interest rates that were specifically designed to deaden the labour market since wage inflation was the central problem of the time. This shift in the policy target associated with interest rate adjustment from the allocation of resources to stopping union wage demands was a necessity of the time, but this is a policy approach whose time has gone.

The supposed "Phillips Curve" relationship between inflation and unemployment has never been demonstrated in modern times. There may well have been such a relationship over the century up until 1958 when Phillips did his original study. There is no evidence today that any such a relationship currently exists.

Third, there then has to be some recognition why there is no apparent inflation in our economies even though money demand continues to increase. There are a number of reasons for this, but I will stick to a couple.

To begin with, we think inflation is subdued because the massive growth in the prices of various asset classes do not get included in our consumer price indexes. House prices have risen at astonishing rates but their increase has hardly troubled the CPI. If housing were properly included, you would get a very different sense of what is going on. My son cannot believe that when we bought our house these many years ago, it cost three times my annual salary at the time. To buy the same house today would now cost ten times his annual salary (twenty times my own), and things are only getting worse. The CPI is now a poor measure of changes in the cost of living for most consumers. Real incomes are lower than our current estimates of prices growth would suggest.

Going beyond this, the private sector remains flat. Outside the public sector, wages growth is minimal. Other than in a handful of protected areas, no one is striking for more money. Most employees find they are falling behind, and see their living standards falling back. Nevertheless, few are about to risk it all on striking for higher pay.

Let me therefore come to the heart of the problem as I see it, and that is the massive increase in public sector spending. GDP growth looks relatively all right because of the increases in the level of either direct public outlays, or in the amount of subsidised "private sector" expenditure that is driven by government demand and subsidy (think green energy).

Our savings are now to an increasing extent in the hands of governments who direct incredible amounts towards what are largely valueless assets. The non-scandal over the National Broadband Network continues to amaze me. A project, literally designed on the back of an envelope during a plane-ride between Melbourne and Sydney, has now blown billions that will never be repaid in value-adding activity. It is a net drain on national savings, and leaves us poorer than we otherwise would have been. But because most look at these issues only in terms of money and not resource depletion – and see only the end product and not the resources being chewed up – there is little general recognition of the harm that has been done. Even if one day we have a fully operational NBN, we will be worse off for the effort than if the project had never been commenced.

Fourth, we have to understand that interest rates can be too low. Market rates of interest below the equilibrium level that equalizes the supply and demand for real savings actually harm the economy. The financial system is designed to determine who will be allowed to deploy our resources. What we need to do is ensure that those who are given command of these resources are those who will create the greatest net value.

Low interest rates misdirect resources towards low-value uses. It may look good to those who do the borrowing, but from a long-term national economic perspective, it is contrary to our future prosperity. If interest rates are high, those with low-valued projects tend to be shut out of the market for credit. The financial system then does its proper job by carefully assessing all of the applicants for these funds to make sure the underlying projects really will provide a positive return.

They often get it wrong, which is why businesses so often fail. For all that, they more usually get it right, which is why our economies continue to grow. Directing our national savings to those who will make the most productive use of those savings is crucial to future prosperity. If, instead, interest rates are kept low, the result is that many more projects will earn a positive return on the funds that are borrowed, but these are projects that will not add as much to our future rates of growth, as the projects that are foregone. Higher rates are a positive feature of a growing economy. Keeping rates low does us no favours.

Fifth, the financial system must be structured so that governments are discouraged from using our resources for their own unproductive purposes. The notion that governments have any idea where the most productive areas of investment are is a conception that really ought to have been discredited years ago. Government-chosen projects, such as those that constituted the stimulus that followed the Global Financial Crisis in 2009, are a fantastic drain on the economy.

Low interest rates may look good to those who buy houses – even though they cause the prices they pay to be higher than they would otherwise have been – but are a massive incentive to governments to borrow for their own purposes and to run deficits *ad infinitum*. A government anyway has the ability to create money by just writing a cheque. Low rates only make it easier for governments to spend. Ultimately, we get to the stage where government debt is just so many pieces of paper. Thus far most economies have not yet turned into Greece, but the potential is always there since the money market seldom puts up its warning signs soon enough

There is a limit to how much money can be poured out relative to the productivity of the economy. There is also a limit on the willingness of a population to see its living standards whittled away. So there is a political limit that is now being tested across the world. What seems to preserve the consensus for the moment is the belief that public spending and low rates of interest are positive steps in generating recovery. Eventually, if only because there is only so much pain that can be withstood, there will be a reaction. How this will play out is anyone's guess, since it is unlikely that the political forces will be ranged in favour of cutting public spending and raising rates. But the pain that is inevitable from following the trajectory we are now on, will eventually need to be faced.

My own preference would be that there be a growing awareness of what a sound policy would look like which would be followed by policy adjustments in those directions. More likely there will be some kind of crescendo that comes with higher rates imposed on our economies in the way it occurred during the 1980s and 1990s. Whether this will be followed by an understanding of what went wrong and what to do ever after, of this I have no confidence at all.

But higher rates must come and the re-adjustment must come immediately after. The pain will almost certainly be intense, but there is no getting our economies on track without first allowing resources to flow where they can earn a positive return.

Some Thoughts on Australia's Recent Monetary Policy Past

Monetary policy under the guidance of Glenn Stevens over the period between 2006 and 2016 should be a guide to future governors of the RBA. It should be, but will only be, if those who take on the role understand the principles that lay behind the actions he took. And, in fact, the principles he applied were in their essentials the ones outlined above. His management of credit policy is one of the reasons the Australian economy continued to grow at reasonable rates even as other economies floundered in the wake of the Global Financial Crisis.

The theoretical structure he applied has its nineteenth century roots in the economic policies of the Swedish economist, Knut Wicksell. The core of the Wicksellian approach to monetary policy was the division of interest rates between "the money rate of interest" – the price of bank credit – and "the natural rate of interest" – the supply and demand for the real capital an economy has available.

The practical result of this approach to policy was the obvious reluctance the RBA had to lowering rates of interest. In spite of the pressure from those who believe low rates promote investment, and from the example set by central banks throughout the rest of the developed world, in Australia interest rates remained relatively high.

Since an economy is the outcome of a blend of policies, each of which has its own particular tug on the totality of what eventuates, there has been little appreciation of the extent to which the Australian economy has benefitted from the maintenance of these somewhat higher rates of interest. Credit comes at a cost. Governments still must pay a positive amount for the funds they borrow.

There has therefore been genuine discrimination within the financial system to separate out the better class of investments from those of lesser value. Governments have also found that borrowing funds has a genuine cost which has to some extent limited the amount that they borrow. Financing public debt is more expensive than it would have been had rates been lower. Public spending has therefore been circumscribed to some extent.

Given the way economic theory is typically framed, there would be almost no appreciation of the momentum that living in a *zero-debt* economy had provided – which is much more than just a balanced budget and were Australia's unique and actual circumstances at the start of the GFC. It is unimaginable that Australia will return to such a situation ever again. Australian governments will be struggling with repayment of debt, which the maintenance of positive rates of interest will continue to constrain. Governments will remain under pressure to reduce debt since the interest cost of this debt will remain an important budget item far into the future.

Beyond the issue of allocating resources within the economy, international interest rate relativities have also been an important consideration. Relatively high rates, when others have managed their rates into very low numbers and even into negative territory, have important exchange rate considerations. It is that one additional factor that has led the RBA to lower rates more than it might otherwise have considered prudent, since the inflow of money to take advantage of these relatively high rates can have effects on Australia's export performance. It is a reminder of the limitations on national economic policy imposed by the decisions made by others.

Thinking about the Future

Economic policy is partly common sense but more importantly determined by the prevailing economic theories of the time. The fact is that the core aim of economic policy is to raise aggregate demand without first raising the real level of aggregate supply, which has led to increased levels of public spending and major cuts in rates of interest. Although these policies have been accompanied by a dismal economic performance, the policies have remained intact because the theory that underpins the actions taken remains virtually unaffected by events.

Australian monetary policy has, however, remained outside the international policy matrix with real rates left higher than in most of the countries of the developed world. Australian economic growth has also remained higher. So far as fiscal policy has gone, Australia followed the same approach as others in trying to regenerate economic growth through increased debt-financed fiscal policies. Only our monetary policy has stood out from the pack. Although the theoretical connection between the superior performance of the Australian economy and the monetary policies that have been pursued by the RBA is underappreciated, it has made an immense difference to how well the economy has travelled. But unless the economic theories explaining why maintaining higher rates of interests helps create the conditions for faster rates of growth are better understood, there will remain the perennial danger that Australia will also start applying easy money policies as a purportedly easy way to return the economy to faster rates of growth.

Australian Energy Policy: the undermining of the nation's interests

Alan Moran

Noted economist and founder of www.regulationeconomics.com

Energy Supply in Australia

Energy plays a crucial role in the Australian economy. Coal accounts for 15 per cent of exports and gas a further 7 per cent. Exports are ostensibly supported by all political parties other than the Greens. However impediments are evident, especially in the laws of standing and regulatory accumulations that are preventing new ventures – most notably the giant Adani coal mine in Queensland.

However, it is the domestic supply of energy in the form of gas and electricity that is the policy focus and cause for greatest concern.

Australia started the present century with a highly competitive electricity supply industry that had become among the cheapest in the world.

Most of the nation had been brought together in a linked National Electricity Market which allowed competition between different generation facilities, many of which had been privatised. This drove down wholesale prices.

Electricity transmission and distribution systems had also been partly privatised and, though their prices were regulated, owners' pursuit of savings and hence profits, drove down costs which became reflected in prices. And retail markets were opened to competition resulting in rivals offering hefty discounts and seeking out new, lower cost supplies.

This beneficial state of affairs stemmed from reforms in the 1990s. Prior to then, electricity had often been used as a feature of industry policy and the industry, fundamentally state government owned, had become grossly overstaffed and managerially inefficient.

Victoria had led the way in establishing a competitive intra-state market followed by privatisations of virtually all electricity and gas assets by 1997. This, once the national market became unified, placed pressure on government owned suppliers to reduce costs, pressure that was intensified by privatisations in South Australia and Queensland.

Prices were reduced for both industry and households. The NUS consultancy estimated residential electricity prices in 2001 as shown in Figure 1.

Figure 1

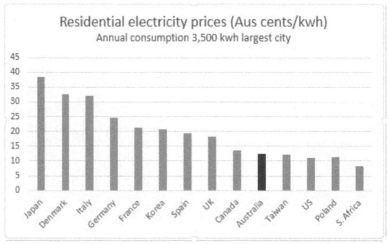

Figure 2

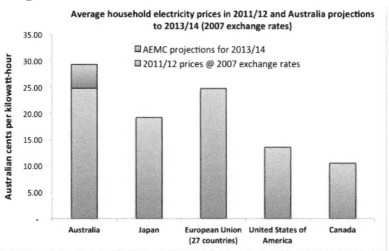

However, by 2014, Australia had slipped down the affordability scale as Figure 2, an assessment conducted for the Australian Parliament, demonstrates.[1]

Gas markets were somewhat less interlinked. Victoria experienced cheap gas as a result of long standing contracts with the Exxon/BHP Bass Strait partners. Other states have been obtaining increasingly available gas supplies from a growing network of pipelines. The pipeline expansion was facilitated by light regulatory controls; the ACCC is however signalling its intention to increase pipeline regulations in the pursuit of fairness, a measure that would dampen investors' enthusiasm to build more facilities.

In eastern Australia, huge gas export plants have been built, causing concern that supplying these will drive up domestic prices. Calls for domestic gas reservation have been frequent, especially in the context of regulatory measures restricting new supplies, but these calls have not found support by either state or Commonwealth governments.

---

[1] http://cmeaustralia.com.au/wp-content/uploads/2013/09/160708-FINAL-REPORT-OBS-INTERNATIONAL-PRICE-COMPARISON.pdf

What went wrong?

The deterioration in Australia's costs was fundamentally due to a resurgence of regulation. Australia's low prices post the 1990s reforms reflected fuel costs. Along the eastern seaboard is among the world's most accessible coal, low in pollutants (nobody until recently classified carbon dioxide as pollutant) and conveniently situated near to markets.

The most significant regulatory intrusion came in the form of renewable energy requirements.

The 2001 Mandatory Renewable Energy Target (MRET) required that 9,500 GWh of selectively designated new renewable energy be used in Australia by 2010. When Prime Minister John Howard announced the proposal to introduce an MRET scheme in 1997 he said it was for an additional two per cent of electricity that was to come from "renewable or specified waste energy". Lobbyists and officials redefined that as 9,500 GWh by 2010, which was in fact far more than "an additional two per cent"; it was, indeed, over four per cent of total projected electricity supply.

A review of the scheme in 2004 (the Tambling Review) recommended the target be increased to 20,000 GWh by 2020. In June 2004 the Commonwealth rejected that, announcing that it did not believe expanding the target was economically justified.

State governments took a contrary view and introduced their own schemes. The Victorian Government announced its proposals in a Press Release by the Premier (2 November 2005)[2] . This argued that there was a "lack of national leadership" by the Federal Government in not increasing the MRET scheme from the 9500 GWh target set. Mr Bracks said this, "is costing Victoria – economically and environmentally – and cannot be allowed to continue." And he set out

---

[2] www.greenhouse.vic.gov.au/images/VicGreenhouse-ActionPlan.pdf

to double "the proportion of renewable energy used by Victorians to 10 per cent by 2010". Mr Bracks said, "Victoria's aim is to facilitate the development of up to 1000 megawatts of wind energy by 2006 represents $2 billion worth of capital investment. Then there are the jobs and the other economic spinoffs that accompany such a significant outlay". One such spin-off, a subsidized blade factory, was closed within a few months.

The Rudd government in 2007 increased the Commonwealth renewables requirements to 20 per cent of total energy by 2020. This was quantified at 45,000 GWh of "exotic" renewables (in addition to the existing 15,000 GWh of commercially provided hydro), though partly due to the energy cost increases stemming from regulatory activity, the 45,000 GWh will exceed the 20 per cent level. The Rudd Government also split the scheme into its present large scale (LRET) at 41,000 GWh and small scale (SRES) categories (mainly rooftop solar) at 4,000 GWh, though there were no disciplines to limit the latter and they have grown to some 12,000 GWh.

In 2014, the Abbott government commissioned the Warburton Inquiry into the renewable energy future. This estimated the cost of the then scheme would be in the range of $20 to $45 billion in the decade to 2020. As a result, the government reduced the level of renewable energy to 33,000 GWh by 2020 bringing total renewable supplies to an estimated 23.5 per cent of the market. This includes commercial hydro at around 8 per cent meaning a 15 per cent share for subsidised renewables.

These subsidised injections of renewable energy have had five outcomes.

First they have resulted in higher overall electricity costs to consumers – the requirements are effected by forcing retailers to include increasing shares of renewable supplies within the total. Wind, the cheapest of the renewables (other than hydro, which cannot be significantly increased) costs around \$110 per megawatt hour, three times the cost of coal fuelled electricity. Moreover, because of its intermittency, wind entails increased balancing costs from other generation sources.

Secondly, wind also incurs higher transmission costs as a result of the dispersed and remote locations of generators. Transmission costs were originally planned to be paid for by generators but are now largely financed by levies on consumers, thereby distorting efficient decisions on plant location and technology.

Thirdly, as has been seen in two severe episodes in South Australia where wind comprises 40 per cent of supply, it is far less reliable than fossil fuel supplies.[3]

Fourthly, because of its subsidised nature wind tends to be bid into the market at near zero prices thereby forcing baseload coal offline, increasing its operating costs and reducing its contribution to meeting capital overhead costs.

Fifthly, the provision of wind power also brings taxpayer costs since it is subsidised by soft loans through the Clean Energy Finance Corporation and other grants.

The renewable industry lobby has put the cost of the investments in renewable energy to achieve these goals at \$40 billion, a sum that provides negative value-added in displacing more efficient supplies. In 2016 renewable subsidies amounted to nearly \$5 billion as shown in Table 1. And the nature of the interventions means a considerable increase in paperburden and associated costs on the part of the energy supply industry, costs that must be recouped from consumers.

---

[3] See *Green, fickle and purely for political gain*, http://media.wix.com/ugd/b6987c_ab68760 65a754caaa9c7bc89f16ebf3c.pdf

Table 1   Estimated greenhouse gas expenditures 2016

Commonwealth Costs 2016 ($M)

LRET costs 21,431,000 MWh at $85	1822
SRES costs 6,000,000 MWh at $40	240
Environment Departmental budget costs	
ARENA	154
CEFC	239
Clean Energy regulator	674
Other	69
Other Agencies (CSIRO, BoM, other depts)	~500
Total Commonwealth	**$698**
Queensland Solar Bonus 350 ($276 per customer in 2015/6)[4]	
NSW Climate Change Fund/Energy Savings	317[5]
ACT	6[6]
Victoria	439[7]
SA	62[8]
State Schemes Total	**$1172**
TOTAL	**$4870**

One upshot has been the gradual closure of coal power stations. As South Australia has the highest level of wind energy at 40 per cent and with plans to progress to 50 per cent, it is unsurprising that its fossil fuel stations were the first to close. Its last coal generator shut its doors in May 2016, just months before the state suffered one near miss and one direct hit in terms of total power outages.

---

[4] http://www.qca.org.au/getattachment/705af491-f002-4a6c-82a1-1a19cefc7f30/Fair-and-Reasonable-Solar-Feed-in-Tariffs-for-Quee.aspx

[5] http://www.environment.nsw.gov.au/resources/grants/150758-climate-change-fund-annual-report-2014-15.pdf

[6] http://www.environment.act.gov.au/energy/cleaner-energy/renewable-energy-target,-legislation-and-reporting/act-large-scale-feed-in-tariff-cost-data

[7] Based on AEMC http://www.aemc.gov.au/getattachment/02490709-1a3d-445d-89cd-4d405b246860/2015-Residential-Electricity-Price-Trends-report.aspx showing Vic schemes twice as costly as NSW

[8] Based on AEMC http://www.aemc.gov.au/getattachment/02490709-1a3d-445d-89cd-4d405b246860/2015-Residential-Electricity-Price-Trends-report.aspx showing SA schemes three times as costly as NSW

The collapse of the South Australian system did not dissuade the Victorian Government from its own resolve to embark upon a similar path. For Victoria the interim goal is 40 per cent renewables by 2025 which would require 2000 wind turbines in addition to the existing 600. The government was surprised and not a little alarmed when, as November came along, the owners of the giant Hazelwood power station announced it would have to close as a result of the favours to renewables and increased taxes on the coal it uses. As a result, Victoria's electricity future prices jumped about 40 per cent and those of the interconnected states also increased.

Government ministers have reacted to the renewable energy induced crisis by calling for more transmission to be built linking state systems. As long as there remains a strong fossil fuel supply this papers over the cracks of systems vulnerable to wind's shortcomings, albeit at some additional expense. And the strategy is available only if fossil fuel powered generators remain operating in the unprofitable conditions created by subsidies to renewables.

In Queensland the government has also embarked upon an ambitious proposal to obtain 50 per cent of its electricity from renewable sources – an especially onerous task since the state is blissfully deficient in wind resources.

In addition to the effects of electricity policy itself, there has been a gradual adverse effect from government buckling to green pressure to prevent the fracking technology being used for gas recovery. This now accounts for the bulk of gas supply in the US but it is virtually completely banned in New South Wales and totally banned – alongside all gas exploration – in Victoria (the initiator of the measure in that state being the Coalition rather than Labor). Such measures have been taken notwithstanding numerous studies and commissions having affirmed that the technology does not cause harm (the main concern being groundwater). Even so, a combination of green activism and farmer anxieties) has arrested the energy source's development.

The various interventions have a compounding effect. This far exceeds the direct costs of substituting 15 per cent of supply by renewables that cost three times the price of the commercial supply they displace. Arithmetically that substitution means an overall cost impact of 30 per cent at the wholesale level and, after taking into account the delivery and retail costs, perhaps only 10-15 per cent price hike in the final bill. However, this is vastly amplified by the dampening effect on investment of commercial energy production and other costs associated with renewable energy. Moreover, a relatively small increase in price has a major effect on industry locational decisions especially for energy intensive industries. We are seeing the aluminium smelters close down, already two of the six operating in 2012 are no longer in production.

Behind the policy moves

Carbon dioxide emissions from fossil fuel burning constitutes two thirds of greenhouse gas emissions.

If, as activists maintain, climate change resulting from emissions of carbon dioxide and other "greenhouse gases" presents cataclysmic prospects for humankind, energy usage must be fundamentally changed.

Those promoting the need for action cite the projections of climate models used by the UN Inter governmental Panel on Climate Change (IPCC) and The Framework Convention on Climate Change. These bodies maintain that a doubling of carbon dioxide and other greenhouse gases in the atmosphere could bring increased global temperatures of up to 5°C, a level that would, it is argued, impose considerable costs on humanity. (Actually the only peer reviewed estimates[9] are for world income, in the event of such climate change, to be less than 5 per cent below the doubling that is expected to take place under business-as-usual).

Moreover, the level of temperature increase has been considerably less than that projected by the models (though in line with the estimates of Lindzen[10] who argues that atmospheric greenhouse gas doubling can only increase global temperatures by 1°C and that most of this has already taken place). Roy Spencer's analysis of models and outcomes below indicates the more sober assessments are closer to the reality.

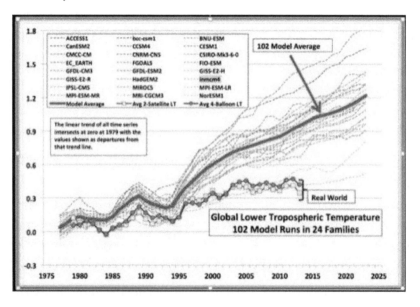

---

[9] Source: D. Arent and R. S. J. Tol, "Chapter 11: Key Economic Sectors and Services," Working Group II contribution to the Fifth Assessment Report, Climate Change 2014: Impacts, Adaptation, and Vulnerability, IPCC (Draft, 2014).

[10] http://impactofcc.blogspot.com.au/2012/02/richard-s-lindzen-reconsidering-climate.html

World and most domestic politicians are unimpressed. In UN meeting after meeting around the world, resolutions are passed, commitments made and measures are adopted that promise action to reduce emissions.

To replace fossil fuel-based sources of power requires unprecedented political change. Not only would it require forcing people within nations into an energy pattern that is vastly more expensive than the current fossil-fuel based systems, but all nations must follow the same path. This requires politicians be vested with vastly augmented powers over their own countrymen and in addition that there must also be a mechanism whereby all nations pursue pretty much the same objective.

For those in the political class, this becomes a mouth-watering prospect for greater influence and wealth. As Prime Minister, Kevin Rudd campaigned strongly for global measures to be taken. His first act as Prime Minister in December 2007 was to ratify the Kyoto Convention under which Australia had undertaken to limit its increase in greenhouse gases to 7 per cent between 1990 and 2012. Mr Rudd famously described anthropogenic global warming as constituting the greatest moral issue of our time.

Even so, to effect this in the context of vastly different costs and benefits from the abatement action would seem to require a Kantian fantasy – a federation of nation states subordinated to some global authority. Fantasy or not, states have indeed adopted economically harmful measures on carbon abatement; even those who actually withdrew, Canada and Japan, took expensive steps to reduce emissions.

Australia achieved its goals partly by its renewable energy policy which was augmented by the carbon tax introduced by the Gillard Government in 2012 (and repealed by the Abbott Government in 2014).

But for Australia, a far more substantial factor was using planning regulations to force landowners not to clear their land for productive use. This resulted in a "saving" of 87.5 million tonnes of greenhouse gases allowing emissions to be kept at around 530 million tonnes[11]. It was effected by combined actions on behalf of the Coalition Government in Canberra (the Minister being Dr David Kemp) and the ALP governments in Queensland and New South Wales. The costs of this were estimated to be $200 billion in devalued land; one landowner who took up the issue, Mr Spencer, saw planning regulations reduce the value of his land from $9 million to a little over $1 million, a sum for which the government offered to buy him out. The planning regulations had a considerable impact on the capacity of the nation to expand its agricultural output, an effect that now appears to entail considerable costs as a result of the expanded demand for agricultural produce from Asia.

Canada considered taking similar action to that of Australia but decided that such a trespass against private property was unconscionable.

These actions by Commonwealth Coalition governments illustrate that the attraction of intervening in the economy to promote (very doubtful) benefits to other nations is not confined to the green and left sides of politics. Although John Howard once out of office declared that the measures he took on climate change were his greatest mistakes he nevertheless took them. And some of his colleagues were and remain enthusiastic supporters of abatement measures and all this entails for costs and national competitiveness.

This was particularly true of the Environment Minister, Greg Hunt, a global warming zealot well before becoming Environment Minister in the Abbott Government. While Prime Minister Abbott

[11] See ABS http://www.abs.gov.au/ausstats/abs@.nsf/Products/4655.0.55.002~2013~Main+Features~Chapter+5+Greenhouse+Gas+Emissions?OpenDocument

himself was a climate skeptic and repealed the carbon tax, he could not or would not do more than the modest 2020 targeted roll-back of renewables from the 41,000 to 33,000 GWh.

As Prime Minister, Tony Abbott presided over the Australian Government's "Intended Nationally Determined Contribution" which was taken to the Paris Agreement on Climate Change adopted in December 2015. Australia undertook to reduce emissions by 26-28 per cent by 2030. That level is similar those adopted by other developed countries, developing countries are however only under obligations to reduce their emissions some 15 years into the future. Developed countries led by the EU, the US and Japan comprise only 35 per cent of global emissions (Australia is about 1.3 per cent) but the Paris Agreement claimed to pave the way to a 2°C limit to global temperatures with aspirational goals of preventing more than 1.5°C.

Is there an exit strategy for Australia?

With developing nations facing no emission disciplines presently emitting 65 per cent of greenhouse gases (a share that is certain to grow) the whole notion that the abatement measures determined upon can have the targeted effect on temperatures makes little sense.

The Paris Agreement would make even less sense if the US were to pull out and, in this respect, its architects were the EU and the Obama administration. Hillary Clinton has vowed to "defend and build on" the Obama Administration's anti-coal regulations and has campaigned on the thousands of jobs allegedly there for the taking with a strong anti-fossil fuel policy. Wikileaks even reported on links between the Clinton campaign and financing of the "lawfare" of the opposition to the $22 billion Adani Queensland coal mine.

By contrast, as President, Donald Trump would dump the US participation in the Paris Agreement and defund the global jamboree that has sponsored it.

Trump has called global warming a hoax and, in quitting the Paris Agreement, would not be impeded from doing so by the four year lock-in that was part of the deal.

Trump would also go full steam ahead in promoting fracking and would cease subsidising renewable energy. A Republican victory in November would offer one silver lining for Australia in the provision of an escape hatch for a deleterious policy seemingly set in stone.

Whether Australia under a Prime Minister rusted-on to the climate change cause would take this exit route in the event of a Trump victory is as uncertain as that victory itself.

Lightning Source UK Ltd.
Milton Keynes UK
UKHW04f1218230718
326136UK00001B/142/P